A Primer of Sōtō Zen

A Primer of Sōtō Zen

A Translation of Dōgen's
Shōbōgenzō Zuimonki
by Reihō Masunaga

丟 *AN EAST-WEST CENTER BOOK*
Published for the East-West Center
by The University Press of Hawaii
Honolulu

First edition 1971
Paperback 1975, 1978

Copyright © 1971 by East-West Center Press
(since July 1971, The University Press of Hawaii)
All rights reserved
Library of Congress Catalog Card Number 76-126044
ISBN 0-8248-0357-4
Manufactured in the United States of America

Contents

Introduction

The *Shōbōgenzō Zuimonki* consists largely of brief talks, hortatory remarks, and instructional and cautionary comments by the Japanese Zen Master Dōgen (1200–1253). These were recorded by his disciple, Ejō (1198–1280), and later edited by the latter's disciples after his death.

The *Shōbōgenzō Zuimonki,* according to the colophon of the popular edition of the Tokugawa period, was compiled during the years 1235–1237, apparently a short time after Dōgen had established his temple, the Kōshōji, at Uji, south of Kyoto. It remained in manuscript form for over four hundred years and was first printed, in a very small edition, in 1651. Later a revised version by Menzan Zuihō (1683–1769), who worked on the text intermittently over a fifty-year period, was published in 1769, although its preface dates to 1758. This edition has become the so-called *rufubon,* the popular text, which is accepted as the standard version of the *Shōbōgenzō Zuimonki.* In 1941 a manuscript copy made in 1644 of an original manuscript of 1380 was discovered at the Chōonji, in Aichi Prefecture. This version, which contains many textual problems, differs considerably from the popular edition in the arrangement of the text, in the items contained, and in the wording; and it may well be much closer in form to the original text. It has recently been published, with a detailed textual study and translation, by Mizuno Mieko in the *Koten Nihon Bungaku Zenshū* series, published by the Chikuma Shobō.

The popular text has seen several modern editions by various scholars. Watsuji Tetsurō (Iwanami), Ōkubo Dōshū (Sankibō), Tamamuro Taijō (Yūzankaku), Tachibana Shundō (Daitō Shuppansha), and Furuta Shōkin (Kadokawa) have all published editions. All of these are based on the popular edition, as revised and edited by Menzan. The present translation is based on Professor Watsuji's version; the division of the six chapters into sections is based also on the method used by Professor Watsuji.

Historically, Dōgen may be called the second priest to have introduced Zen to Japan. Meditation practices had played an important role in the older sects of Japanese Buddhism, and Zen priests had come to Japan in earlier periods, but they had established no temples and started no schools. Eisai (1131–1215) had brought the Rinzai Zen teachings to Japan and was the first to establish a Zen temple in that country, but he met with much opposition from the traditional schools, who were not sympathetic to the establishment of a rival school of Buddhism. Dōgen studied for many years in China under a Sōtō Zen Master, Ju-ching (1163–1228), and it was his teaching that Dōgen brought back, although he himself made no attempt to establish a sect of Zen. After Dōgen, many Japanese priests visited the China of the Sung and Yüan dynasties, and Chinese priests came to Japan, bringing with them the teachings of a variety of Chinese Zen Masters.

The *Shōbōgenzō Zuimonki* does not give the full scope of Dōgen's thought. For this, one must look to his monumental *Shōbōgenzō.* This work, as well as the *Shōbōgenzō Zuimonki,* was unusual in terms of the times in which it was written, in that it was composed in the Japanese language rather than in Chinese. Up to this time, Japanese Buddhists had all written in Chinese, and the collected records of the many Zen Masters who followed Dōgen continued to be written in this language until the Tokugawa period. The *Shōbōgenzō* is a difficult work, involving many textual and doctrinal problems that are yet to be resolved, but there is no room here to examine the complexities of this work.

The *Shōbōgenzō Zuimonki* does not concern itself with any great philosophical subtleties, and yet it gives an insight into the type of Buddhism that Dōgen sought to propagate as well as the essential requirements that Dōgen found imperative for a successful conduct of the monastic life. Very often Dōgen's comments are directed towards the beginner in Zen and towards lay followers. They are designed to point out to the disciples under him the emotional and physical climate necessary to the successful pursuit of their efforts. He described the perils of the transient world and the degenerate age in which his disciples lived. He urged them to develop the mind that seeks the Way, to forsake all worldly commitments, and to practice Buddhism for the sake of Buddhism alone.

repetitive like Nishioas work

Very often the work is repetitive. We can imagine that Dōgen dwelt often on the same subjects to insure that his lessons were impressed on his hearers' minds. Such repetitions are inevitable in a work that is recorded by a disciple and is not a document written consciously for publication and distribution. Often there are inconsistencies. At times the followers are exhorted to follow the conduct of their predecessors in Zen; at times they are cautioned to ignore them. Such inconsistencies develop in part, perhaps, from the different levels from which Dōgen talks: at times he is the mentor to virtual beginners, and his approach is the simple one that explains the requisites for study; occasionally, he is the accomplished Zen Master, who has transcended all dualisms, and he speaks from the level of that accomplishment. Although this problem is not met with to any great degree in the *Shōbōgenzō Zuimonki,* it is often a trap for the unwary reader that is to be found in most Zen writings, since the standpoint from which the Master speaks is frequently difficult to ascertain. ✶

The *Shōbōgenzō Zuimonki,* since its publication in its revised form by Menzan, has gained considerable popularity, especially in modern times, when scholars and religious leaders have, in a manner of speaking, "taken up" Dōgen and have published numerous editions of his works. Dōgen's writings require further study, but the *Shōbōgenzō Zuimonki* remains as a first-hand, non-sectarian introduction to the prerequisites for the study of Zen, as seen by a great Zen Master, who studied long and successfully under the strict but compassionate tutelage of a Chinese teacher of Zen.

I

1

One day Dōgen instructed:

In the *Hsü kao-seng chuan*,[1] there is a story about a monk in the assembly of a certain Zen Master. The monk always carried around with great reverence a golden image of the Buddha and other relics. Even when in the dormitory, he constantly burned incense to them and showed his respect with salutations and offerings.

One day the Zen Master said: "The Buddha image and relics that you are worshipping will be of no use to you later." The monk disagreed with him, but the Master continued: "This is the handiwork of demons. Throw them away." The monk grew indignant and started to leave, but the Zen Master called after him. "Open your box and look inside." When the enraged monk complied, he is said to have found a poisonous snake coiled within.

As I see it, relics should be reverenced, since they represent the Tathāgata's image and his remaining bones. It is wrong, however, to expect enlightenment just by worshipping them. This is an error that delivers you into the hands of demons and poisonous snakes. The Buddha's teaching has established the merit of practicing reverence so that the image and relics offer the same blessings to men and devas as does the living Buddha. It is quite true that, if you revere and make offerings to the World of the Three Treasures,[2] you eradicate your crimes, gain merit, remove the karma that leads to rebirth in the evil realms,[3] and are rewarded with birth as man or deva. But it is a mistake to think that you can gain enlightenment in this way.

Since the true disciple follows the Buddha's teaching and seeks to attain the Buddha's rank directly, you must devote

all your efforts to practice in accordance with these teachings
The true practice that accords with these teachings is
concentrated *zazen,* the most essential element in the Zen
monastery today. Think this over well.

2

Dōgen also said:

Although the precepts and the eating regulations should be
maintained, you must not make the mistake of establishing
them as of primary importance and of basing your practice
on them; nor should they be considered a means to
enlightenment. Since they suit the conduct of the Zen monk
and the style of the true disciple, they are observed. To say
that they are good, however, does not make them the most
essential teaching. This does not mean that you should break
the precepts and become dissolute, but, if you attach to them,
your view is wrong and you depart from the Way.

The precepts and eating regulations are maintained
because they follow Buddhist ritual and represent a monastery
style. At the time I lived in the monasteries in China, they did
not seem to play the major role in the daily lives of the monks.
To attain the True Way, you must practice the *zazen* and *kōan*
meditation as handed down by the Buddhas and the
Patriarchs. Gogembō,[4] a fellow student at Kenninji and a
disciple of the late Abbot Eisai,[5] when he was at a Zen temple
in China, adhered strictly to the eating regulations and
recited the *Precept Sutra*[6] day and night. I instructed him
concerning the above, and he gave up this practice.

Ejō asked: "Should the regulations established by
Po-chang[7] be followed in the Zen monastery? In the beginning
of these regulations, one reads: 'To receive and guard the
precepts is of primary importance.' The precepts handed
down today seem to teach the basic precepts transmitted
from the Buddhas and the Patriarchs. In the oral transmission
from teacher to disciple of Zen, the precepts transmitted
from the West[8] are taught to the students. These are the
Bodhisattva precepts of today, and in the *Precept Sutra* one
reads that they must be chanted night and day. Why then do
you want us to stop chanting them?"

Dōgen said: "What you say is right. Students should guard

with special care the regulations laid down by Po-chang. These rules call for receiving and obeying the precepts and for practicing *zazen*. Chanting the *Precept Sutra* day and night and strictly obeying the precepts is simply to practice concentrated *zazen,* as did the Zen Masters of old. When doing *zazen,* what precepts are not upheld, what merits not produced? The actions of the ancient Zen Masters all have a most profound meaning. Without holding personal views, just go along with the assembly and practice, trusting in the actions of the old Masters."

3
Once Dōgen instructed: [9]

A monk studying with Fo-chao ch'an-shih[10] became ill and decided he wanted some meat to eat. Fo-chao granted him permission. One night Fo-chao went to the infirmary and watched the sick monk eating meat in the dim light. A demon, perched on his head, was eating the meat, although the monk thought he was putting it into his own mouth. From that time on the Zen Master knew that, when the convalescent monk wanted to eat meat, it would be taken away from him by a demon; so he allowed him to have meat.

In a matter such as this you should exercise judgment whether meat eating should be allowed or not. A similar problem arose among the followers of Wu-tsu Fa-yen.[11] How this matter was settled depended on the inclination of the Zen Master concerned.

4
One day Dōgen instructed:

You should understand that a man who is born into a certain household and wants to enter the family occupation must first train himself in the family specialty. It is a mistake to strive for knowledge and training in an area outside your own specialty and competence.

Now, as men who have left your homes, if you are to enter the Buddha's house and become priests, you must learn thoroughly what you are supposed to do. To learn these things and to maintain the regulations mean to cast aside attachments to the Self and to conform to the teachings of the

Zen Masters. The essential requisite is to abandon avarice. To do this, you must first free yourselves from egoism. To be free from egoism is to have a deep understanding of transiency. This is the primary consideration.

Most people in the world like to regard themselves as good and to have others think the same of them, but such a thing seldom happens. If, however, you gradually forsake attachment to the Self and follow the advice of your teacher, you will progress. You may say that you understand but still cannot give up certain things; and practice *zazen* while holding on to various attachments. If you take this attitude, you sink into delusion.

For a Zen monk the primary prerequisite for improvement is the practice of concentrated *zazen*. Without arguing about who is clever and who inept, who is wise and who foolish, just do *zazen*. You will then naturally improve.

5

Dōgen instructed:

Nothing can be gained by extensive study and wide reading. Give them up immediately. Just focus your mind on one thing, absorb the old examples, study the actions of former Zen Masters, and penetrate deeply into a single form of practice. Do not think of yourself as someone's teacher or as someone's predecessor.

6

Once Ejō asked: "What is meant by the expression: 'Cause and effect are not clouded'?"[12]

Dōgen said: "Cause and effect are immovable."

Ejō asked: "If this is so, how can we escape?"

Dōgen replied: "Cause and effect emerge clearly at the same time."

Ejō asked: "If this is so, does cause prompt the next effect, or does effect bring about the next cause?"

Dōgen said: "If everything were like that, it would be like Nan-ch'üan cutting the cat.[13] Because the assembly was unable to say anything, Nan-ch'üan cut the cat in two. Later, when Nan-ch'üan told this story to Chao-chou,[14] the latter put his straw sandal on his head and went out, an excellent performance. If I had been Nan-ch'üan, I would have said: 'Even if you can speak, I will cut the cat, and even if you cannot speak, I will still cut it. Who is arguing about the cat? Who can save the cat?' Or else I would have said for the assembly: 'We cannot say, Master. Please cut the cat.' Then again I might have said: 'You know how to cut the cat in two with one sword, but you don't know how to cut the cat in one with one sword.' "

Ejō asked: "What is cutting the cat in one with one sword?"

Dōgen replied: "The cat itself. When the assembly could not reply and if I had been Nan-ch'üan, I would have released the cat, since the assemblage had already said they could not answer.[15] An old Master has said: 'In expressing full function, there are no fixed methods.' "[16]

Dōgen continued: "This 'cutting of the cat' is an expression of full function in Buddhism. It is a pivot word.[17] If it were not, mountains, rivers, and the great sea could not be said to be mind, unexcelled, pure, and clear. Nor could one then say: 'This very mind is Buddha.' Immediately upon hearing this pivot word, see the cat itself as the Buddha body. Upon hearing this word, students should suddenly gain enlightenment."

Dōgen said: "Cutting the cat is an action of a Buddha."

Ejō asked: "What should we call this action?"

Dōgen said: "Call it cutting the cat."

Ejō asked: "Would this be a crime?"

Dōgen said: "It would."

Ejō asked: "Then how can we escape from this crime?"

Dōgen said: "The action of the Buddha and the crime are separate, but they both occur at once in one action.[18]

Ejō asked: "Is this what is meant by the prātimokṣa precepts?"[19]

Dōgen said: "Yes, but while such a view[20] is all right, it would be better not to hold it."

Ejō asked: "Does the phrase 'violating the precepts' refer to crimes committed after receiving the precepts, or can it refer to crimes committed before receiving them?"

Dōgen replied: "The phrase 'violating the precepts' applies to crimes committed after receiving the precepts. Crimes committed before receiving the precepts can be called 'sinful' or 'evil actions,' but not 'violating the precepts.' "

Ejō asked: "Within the forty-eight minor precepts,[21] the term 'violation' is applied to crimes committed before receiving the precepts. Why is this?"

Dōgen replied: "This is not so. It applies to a person who has not yet received the precepts but is about to receive them and repents the crimes he has committed up to then. To receive the ten precepts,[22] he says 'violated' for each instance that his actions in the past have run counter to the forty-eight precepts. Crimes committed beforehand are not considered to have 'violated the precepts.' "

Ejō asked: "The *Sūtra* states that, when someone seeks to receive the precepts and repents the sins he has committed before, he be taught to recite the ten major precepts and the forty-eight minor precepts. In a later passage, however, the *Sūtra* states that the precepts should not be explained to those who have not received them. What is the difference between the two?"

Dōgen replied: "Receiving the precepts and reciting the precepts differ. For repentance, reciting the *Precept Sutra* is like concentrating the mind on the sutras. Therefore, even one who has not received the precepts wants to recite the *Precept Sutra*. There can be no objection to explaining the *Precept Sutra* to him. A later passage forbids teaching it for profit to those who have as yet not received the precepts. It should be taught particularly to those who have received the precepts in order to help them to repent."

Ejō asked: "In receiving the precepts, they are not supposed to be given to anyone who has committed the seven grave sins,[23] yet in the *Sūtra* it is written that even grave sins should be repented. Why is this?"

Dōgen replied: "They should indeed be repented. The proscription against such people receiving the precepts is in the sense of a temporary check.[24] The previous passage in the text states that even a person who violates the precepts, should he repent and then receive the precepts again, becomes pure. If he repents, he becomes pure. This is different from not yet having received the precepts."

Ejō asked: "If repentance of the seven grave sins is allowed, is it permissable to receive the precepts afterwards?"

Dōgen answered: "Yes. This is a custom established by the late Abbot Eisai. Once a person's repentance has been accepted, he must receive the precepts again. Even in the case of the grave sins, anyone who repents should be permitted to receive the precepts again if he so desires. Should even a Bodhisattva himself violate the precepts, he must be given the precepts again, since he has done this for the sake of others."

7

In an evening talk Dōgen said:

Monks must not be scolded and castigated with harsh words; nor should they be held up to scorn by having their faults pointed out. Even if they are evil men, they must not be despised and abused. No matter how bad they may seem at first, when more than four persons gather together for practice, they constitute a *sangha,* which enriches the country. They are deserving of the utmost respect. If your disciples are in error, whether they be temple priests or senior priests, Masters, or teachers, you should instruct and guide them with compassion and kindness. Strike those who have to be struck, scold those who have to be scolded, but do not allow yourself to utter words of slander and detraction. My former teacher Ju-ching,[25] when he was priest of the temple at Mount T'ien-t'ung, would strike the monks with his slipper to keep them from dozing during *zazen* sessions in the meditation hall and would revile and scold them. Yet the assembled monks were glad to be hit, and praised him for it.

Once, after having delivered a lecture, he said: "I have grown old, retired from the assembly, and now live in a small temple and nourish this old body of mine. Yet, being the teacher to the assembly, I serve as the head priest of this small temple so that I may destroy the delusions of each one of you and teach you the Way. That's why I sometimes use words of rebuke; and I sometimes strike you with my bamboo rod. But I really have no heart for it. Nevertheless, I use these instruction methods standing in the place of the Buddha. Monks, permit this with compassion." When Ju-ching finished, the assembled monks all wept.

All of you should teach and guide in this manner. Just

because you hold the rank of head of a temple or senior priest, you have no right to insult the assembled monks, rashly ordering them around as though they were your own belongings. How much more of an error is it then to pick on somebody's weak point and criticize him for it when you yourself hold no such high position! Be very careful about this.

If you see the weaknesses of others and consider these bad and if you wish to guide such people with compassion, you must do so without speaking directly of their errors so that you do not arouse their anger.

8

Dōgen once told this story:

When the late General of the Left of Kamakura (Minamoto Yoritomo)[26] was a youth known as Hyōenosuke, he attended a special banquet one day near the Imperial Palace. As he took his place near the Chief State Councillor, a guest became disorderly, and the Councillor ordered Yoritomo to arrest the man.

Yoritomo refused: "Give your order to Rokuhara,"[27] he said. "He is the general of the Taira family."

The State Councillor said: "But you are here right now."

Yoritomo replied, "I am not qualified to arrest the man."

These words of Yoritomo are admirable, indeed. It was with this attitude that he later ruled the country. Students today should emulate him. Don't rebuke others if you are not in a position to do so.

9

In an evening talk Dōgen said:

There was once a general named Lu Chung-lien,[28] who served P'ing-yüan Chün[29] and subdued the enemies of the Court. When P'ing-yüan praised his skill and sought to reward him with much gold and silver, Lu declined, saying: "A general's duty is to subdue the enemy; it is not to gain praise and possessions." Lu Chung-lien's selflessness and integrity are well known.

Thus, even among laymen, the wise are aware of their responsibilities and perform their functions to the fullest.

They seek no special rewards. Students should be careful to do the same. Upon entering Buddhism they should work for Buddhism without thought of gain. The various teachings, both Buddhist and non-Buddhist, all admonish against acquiring possessions.

10

Once, after a discussion of the doctrine, Dōgen instructed:

It is not good to overwhelm another person with argument even when he is wrong and you are right. Yet it is also not right to give up too easily, saying, "I am wrong," when you have every reason to believe that you yourself are right. The best way is to drop the argument naturally, without pressing the other person or falsely admitting that you yourself are wrong. If you don't listen to his arguments and don't let them bother you, he will do the same and not become angry. This is something to watch carefully.

11

Dōgen instructed:

In the swift march of transiency, birth and death are vital matters. During this short life, if you want to practice and study, just practice and study Buddhism. Writing prose and poetry is, in the long run, useless; thus, it should be given up. When studying and practicing Buddhism, do not take up too many outside things. Be sure to keep away from the scriptural teachings of the sects of esoteric and exoteric Buddhism. Even the *Records* of the Zen Patriarchs should not be studied on too wide a scale. The dull and inferior person finds it hard to concentrate even on one thing. How much more difficult is it for him to do many things at the same time and still keep his mind and thoughts in harmony!

12

Dōgen instructed:

There is a story about how the Zen Master Chih-hsüeh,[30] some centuries ago, conceived the desire to seek the Way and become a Zen monk. Originally a government official, he was gifted with great intelligence and had a reputation for honesty and wisdom. Once, while he was serving as a provincial governor, he appropriated public money and gave it to the people. One of his associates reported this to the Throne. When the Emperor heard the story, he was astounded; and his ministers were similarly puzzled by Chih-hsüeh's action. However, his crime was a serious one, and the death penalty was pronounced.

The Emperor discussed the problem with his ministers, saying: "Here is a talented and wise official. He must have had some special motive for committing this crime. Perhaps he acted from some deep inner reason. If he looks regretful when his neck is about to be cut, cut it off quickly. If he has no such look on his face, he must certainly have some deeper motive. In that case, don't let him die."

When the Imperial Messenger brought out Chih-hsüeh and his neck was about to be cut, he had indeed no look of regret but instead wore an expression of joy on his face. Chih-hsüeh said: "I dedicate my life in this birth to all living beings."

The Imperial Messenger was amazed and reported this to the Emperor. "It is just as I thought," said the Emperor. "He must have had a deeper motive. I thought so from the beginning." The Emperor then requested an explanation.

Chih-hsüeh said: "I've been thinking of retiring from my government post, abandoning my life, giving alms, and of associating myself with sentient beings everywhere. I intend to be reborn as a monk and single-mindedly practice Buddhism." The Emperor was impressed and permitted him to become a monk. He gave him the name Yen-shou (Prolonged Life) to celebrate his reprieve from execution. Monks today should arouse a similar attitude at least once. They should be ready to sacrifice their lives, deepen the feeling of compassion for all living beings, and give rise to the desire to entrust their bodies to the Buddha Way. If they have even a trace of such a feeling, they should protect it against loss. Unless they can arouse such feelings at least once, it will be impossible to awaken to Buddhism.

13

In an evening talk Dōgen said:

The purpose of awakening to the old stories of the Patriarchs of Zen is to modify gradually what you have understood and thought up to now, under the guidance of a Zen Master. Even if the Buddha you have known up to now is endowed with the distinguishing marks,[31] radiates light, and has, like Śākyamuni and Amita Buddha, the virtue of preaching sermons and bringing benefit to the people, you must believe it if the Zen Master tells you that the Buddha is a toad or an earthworm. You will have to give up the beliefs you have held up to now. But if you seek the Buddha's marks, his radiance, and the various virtues associated with him on the earthworm, you still have not modified your arbitrary views of the Buddha. Just recognize as the Buddha what you see now before your eyes. If you follow the words of the Zen Master and turn from deluded views and attachments, you will accord naturally with the Buddha Way.

Yet students today cling to their deluded views and hold on to their personal ideas, thinking that the Buddha is this thing or that thing. If these things differ from what they imagine, they deny that this can be and wander lost, looking for something similar to what their deluded ideas are. They make scarcely any progress along the Buddha Way.

When told to let go of both hands and feet, after climbing to the top of a hundred-foot pole, and then to advance one step further without regard for their own bodies,[32] they say: "It is only because I am alive today that I have the chance to study Buddhism." They are not really following their teacher. This must be understood thoroughly.

14

In an evening talk Dōgen said:

People in this world often try to study many things at the same time and, as a result, do nothing well. They should instead learn one thing so well that they can do it even in front of a crowd. Buddhism, which transcends the ordinary world, is a doctrine that from the beginningless beginning has never been easily learned.[33] This is still so today. Our capacity for study is also limited. In the endlessly high and wide sphere of Buddhism, if we try to learn many aspects, we cannot master even one. Even if he devotes himself to one thing only, a person with inferior capacity finds it difficult to get much done in one lifetime. Students must concentrate on one thing alone.

Ejō asked: "If this is so, what kind of practice should be undertaken? What aspect among the Buddhist teachings should we concentrate our practice on?"

Dōgen replied: "It depends upon the student's talent and capability, but in Zen the practice that has been handed down by the Patriarchs is essentially *zazen. Zazen* is suitable for all people, whether their capacities be superior, mediocre, or inferior.

"When I was in China in the assembly under Ju-ching, I became aware of this truth and thereafter practiced *zazen* day and night. Many monks gave up when it was very cold or very hot, fearing that they would get sick. But at these times I thought to myself: 'Even if I get sick and die, I must just practice *zazen*. If I do not train while I am healthy, what use is this body of mine? If I get sick and die, then that will be my fate. What more can I ask than to study under a Zen Master in the great Sung China, die here, and have the good monks bury me? If I were to die in Japan, such superior priests would not attend my funeral. If I practice but die before gaining enlightenment, I am sure that my next life will be that of a Buddhist follower. A long life without practice seems pointless. Of what use would it be? After so much concern for protecting my body against illness, what a pity it would be if I were to drown accidentally at sea or encounter some other unexpected death.' These were the thoughts that passed through my mind as I sat day and night in earnest effort. As it was, I never once became sick.

"Each of you should practice with utmost diligence. Out of ten of you, all ten should gain enlightenment. My late Zen Master, Ju-ching, encouraged his monks in this way."

15

Dōgen instructed:

It is easy enough to give up one's life or to slice off one's flesh, hands, or feet if one feels so inclined. Similarly, in worldly affairs the same thing can be done because of an attachment to fame and profit. But it is difficult to harmonize

---

the mind as it comes into contact with events and things. When students conceive the desire to discard their lives, they should calm their minds for a while. They should consider whether what they have to say or do conforms to the truth; if it does, then they should say and do it.

16
Dōgen instructed:

Students of the Way must not worry about clothing or food. They must merely follow the Buddhist rules and not concern themselves with worldly things. The Buddha said: "For clothing, use tattered cast-aside garments; for food, use what can be begged." In any kind of world these two things will not be exhausted. Don't forget the swiftness of change, nor let yourself be needlessly troubled by worldly affairs. While in this brief dewlike existence, think only of Buddhism, and don't concern yourself with any other problems.

Somebody asked: "Although fame and profit are said to be hard to cast aside, they are great obstacles to practice and thus must be given up. For this reason I have done so. Although clothing and food are small things, they are important to the practicer. To wear a tattered robe and beg for food are the marks of a superior monk. This was the custom in India. In the temples of China the monks share utensils and belongings in common so that they have no need to worry about them. In the temples of Japan there are no such belongings, and the custom of begging for food has, for the most part, not been transmitted. Under these conditions, what can an inferior and weak person do? If someone like me seeks offerings from believers, he is guilty of receiving donations that he is not entitled to receive. It is improper for us to eat food gained by doing the work of farmers, merchants, warriors, or craftsmen. Yet if everything is left to fate, we seem to get the most meager share. When hunger and cold come, we worry and find our practice impeded. Somebody gave me the following advice: 'Your way of doing things is all wrong. You seem totally unaware of the times and circumstances in which we life. We are born inferior and live in a degenerate age. Your type of training will lead only to retrogression. Make arrangements with a parishioner, or obtain a pledge from a patron; and then you can retire in security to a quiet place where you can peacefully practice Buddhism without worrying about food and clothing. This is not coveting wealth and property. You can then practice with your means of livelihood assured for a while.' I listened to what he said but don't believe him. Just what attitude should one take?"

Dōgen answered: "The conduct of the Zen monk is only to study the style of the Buddhas and Patriarchs. Although India, China, and Japan differ, true students of the Way have never behaved in the manner you describe. Just don't let your mind cling to worldly affairs but study the Way with single-mindedness. The Buddha has said: 'Possess nothing except your robes and bowl and give to starving people the leftovers from what you have begged.' If not a scrap is to be saved from what you receive, how much more so should one avoid rushing about searching for things.

"In a non-Buddhist work it is said: 'In the morning hear the Way, in the evening die content.'[34] Even if you should die from hunger and cold, follow the Buddhist teaching if even for one day or for just one moment. In ten thousand *Kalpa*s and one thousand lives, how many times are we born and how many times do we die! All this comes from our deluded clinging to the world. If just once in this life, we have followed the Buddhist teachings and then starved to death, we have truly attained to eternal peace.

"In fact, I have not read in all the Buddhist scriptures of a single Buddha or Patriarch in India or China or Japan who died of hunger or cold. In this world there is an allotted share of clothing and food for each person while he is alive. It is not obtained by seeking, nor does one fail to obtain it even if one does not seek it. Just leave it to fate and do not let it trouble you. If you say that this is a degenerate age and do not arouse the mind that seeks the Way in this life, in what life do you expect to gain it? Even if you are not a person such as Subhūti or Mahākāśyapa,[35] you should study the Way in accordance with your capacity.

"A non-Buddhist text says: 'Those who like beautiful women will like a woman even though she is not as beautiful as Hsi Shih or Mao Ch'iang.[36] Those who like fine horses will like a horse even if it is not as fine as Fei-t'u or Lu-erh.[37] Those who like fine flavors will enjoy the taste even if it is not dragon's liver or phoenix marrow.'[38] It is just a matter of each expressing his own inclination. This is so among laymen and applies to the followers of Buddhism as well.

"Did not even the Buddha offer twenty years of his life for our benefit in this degenerate age![39] Because of this, offerings by men and devas are still being made to Zen monasteries. Even though the Tathāgata possessed supernatural powers of the greatest merit, he had to eat grain meant for horses[40] to get through one rainy season.[41] How can disciples in this degenerate age want things easier?"

Someone asked: "Instead of violating the precepts, vainly receiving donations from men and deva, wasting the Tathāgata's legacy without arousing the mind that seeks the Way, would it not be better to be like laymen, do the kind of work they do, and practice the Way while we are alive?"

Dōgen said: "Who said to break the precepts and be without the mind that seeks the Way? All you should do is to arouse this mind and practice Buddhism with diligence. It is said that the Tathāgata's blessings are received equally whether the precepts are observed or violated, whether a person is just starting in the Way or has practiced it a long time. Nothing says that, if you violate the precepts, you should return to lay life; or that, if you are without the mind that seeks the Way, you should not practice. Who has this mind in the beginning? It is just that if what is hard to arouse is aroused, if what is hard to practice is practiced, you will undoubtedly make progress. Every man possesses the Buddha-nature. Do not demean yourselves.

"The *Wen-hsüan* says: 'A nation prospers because of one man. The way of the ancient sages is destroyed by the fools that follow.'[42] These words mean that, if one sage comes forth in a nation, that nation prospers; if one fool comes forth, the way of the sages declines. Consider this well."

17
During a talk on a variety of subjects Dōgen said:
When ordinary men and women get together, whether young or old, they very often chat about things of a most

improper nature. This diverts their minds and makes for lively conversation. It gives them enjoyment and serves to alleviate boredom, but this kind of talk is expressly forbidden for monks. Even among laymen, it rarely occurs when good, sober, and courteous people gather to discuss serious problems. Usually it is associated with drunkenness and dissipation. Monks must concentrate on Buddhism alone. Indecent talk is indulged in only by a few confused and eccentric monks.

In the temples of China there is no such problem, since the monks do not engage in trivial talk. Even in Japan, while Eisai, the Abbot of Kenninji, was still alive, such talk was never engaged in. Even after his death, while a few of his disciples were still at the temple, there was virtually no idle conversation. In the past seven or eight years, however, some of the younger people have started to engage in small talk. A most regrettable affair.

Within the Buddhist teachings, it is written that violent words sometimes lead people to enlightenment but that worthless conversation obstructs the True Way. When even words that come spontaneously to the lips and useless theories are obstacles to the Way, how much more likely is it that indecent talk will incite the mind. You must be very careful about this. Not only must you consciously refrain from talk of this sort, but, knowing that something is bad, you must also gradually learn to cast it aside.

18

In an evening talk Dōgen said:

Most laymen like to publicize their good deeds and hide the bad ones. Since such an attitude is repugnant to the guardian deities,[43] good acts go unrewarded, and bad acts, done in secret, are punished. This gives the impression that there is no reward for good deeds and that Buddhism has little benefit to offer. This view is wrong, of course, and must be corrected by all means.

You should secretly do good when no one is watching, and, if you do wrong, you should confess and repent. In this way good acts done in secret will be rewarded. Open confession of wrongdoing removes the crime so that benefits naturally accrue in this present world and in future worlds as well.

A layman in the audience came up and asked: "Nowadays, when laymen give offerings to monks and take refuge in Buddhism, much misfortune is apt to result. They become prejudiced and do not wish to rely on the Three Treasures. What about this?"

Dōgen answered: "This isn't the fault of the monks or of Buddhism, but it is the laymen themselves who are in error. This is why: you may respectfully make offerings to monks who seem to uphold the precepts, follow the eating regulations, and practice strict discipline; yet you do not give to monks who brazenly violate the precepts, drink wine, and eat meat because you consider them unworthy. A mind that discriminates in this way clearly violates the principles of Buddhism. Therefore, even if you take refuge in Buddhism, there is no merit and no response. The precepts contain several passages that caution against just this attitude. When you meet a monk, make offerings to him, regardless of his virtue or lack of it. By all means, avoid trying to judge his inner virtue by his outward appearance.

"In these degenerate times, there are indeed monks whose appearance is scarcely presentable, but there are other monks whose thoughts and actions are infinitely worse. Do not differentiate between good and bad, but render respect to anyone if he is a disciple of the Buddha. If you make offerings and show reverence impartially, you will always be following the Buddha's will and will at once gain benefits.

"Remember the four phrases: 'Action unseen, reward unseen; action unseen, reward seen; action seen, reward unseen; and action seen, reward seen.' Reward for what you do in this life can be gained in this life, the next life, or in some future life. Study this principle well."

19

In a talk one evening Dōgen said:

Supposing someone comes to you to talk about his affairs and asks you to write a letter soliciting a favor or aiding him in a lawsuit. Do you refuse him to his face, saying: "I am now a monk who has retired from the world and have no business concerning myself with mundane affairs?" This must be considered carefully in terms of the time and the occasion.

While this may seem to be the proper attitude for a monk to take, if you think about it, what you are really saying is: "I am a monk who has retired from the world, and if I say something that I have no business saying, I will probably be thought ill of." This shows an attachment to the Self and a concern about one's own fame. At a time like this, think the matter over thoroughly, and if you can help the man even slightly, do so without worrying about what others will think of you. If the friend who receives the letter is offended, feeling that you have behaved in a way unbecoming a monk, is it so bad to lose the friendship of someone who understands so little? Your primary concern inwardly is to free yourself from egoistic attachments and thoughts of your own name, even though outwardly you are doing something quite unbecoming your position.

When someone asks a Buddha or a Bodhisattva for help, they are willing to offer their own flesh and limbs. Why then turn away someone who comes to ask you to write one letter just because you are afraid of what people will say? This just shows how deep your attachment to the Self is. Even if people criticize your actions as unbecoming a monk, if you help others even a little bit and have no desire yourself for fame or profit, you are following the True Way. There are many examples of this sort of behavior among the sages of old. I have done the same myself. It's a simple thing to do a small favor by writing a letter for someone who requests it, even though it might upset your parishioners and friends.

Ejō said: "What you say is quite true. It's all right to ask for something good that will benefit others. But what would you say if the request might cause another person to have his belongings taken away or have something bad happen to him? Should such a request be transmitted?"

Dōgen replied: "It's not for us to decide whether the request is good or bad. It's a good idea, though, to tell the person who asks for the letter and to add in the letter itself that you are writing on that person's request and that you yourself have no knowledge of the merits of his case. The person who gets the letter should be able to judge for himself. These are things we know nothing about, and there is no point in our distorting things by talking to him about them. Supposing you are asked to make a request that you know to be bad of a friend who thinks highly of you and has the utmost faith in your judgment. In that event, write the unpleasant things with which you do not agree exactly in the way that you heard them from the other person. And add that the person to whom the letter is addressed should use his own discretion and handle things as he sees fit. If it is done in this way, no one will have cause for regret. These are things that occur when you meet people or when special circumstances arise; hence, they must be thought over thoroughly. The main point is that, whatever the situation, you must discard attachments to fame and the Self."

20
In a talk one evening Dōgen said:
In this world, both laymen and monks tend to publicize their good deeds and hide the bad ones. Because of this, their inner and outer lives do not correspond. They should try somehow to bring together their inner and outer selves, repent their mistakes, hide their true inner virtues, refrain from adorning their outward appearance, credit others with the good things they have done, and take the blame for bad things others have done.

Someone said: "As you say, we should try to hide our true inner virtue and refrain from outward show. It is basic that the Buddha and Bodhisattvas show a great compassion for the sake of all living things. If ignorant monks and laymen see a nondescript priest, they may be insulting or critical and thus invite the retribution due for slandering a priest. Without knowing the true inner virtue of a priest, laymen sometimes reverently make donations because of the outward appearance and think that this will bring them blessings. What do you think about this?"

Dōgen answered: "To say that one will refrain from outward show and then just act arbitrarily is also against reason.

To say that one will not outwardly show his true virtue and then to behave badly in front of laymen is clearly a serious violation of the precepts. There are those who try to create the impression that they themselves are Buddhists possessed of seldom-seen accomplishments or who try to conceal their defects, but the eyes of the guardian deities and the Three Treasures penetrate everywhere. You are cautioned not to possess a mind that shamelessly seeks for the veneration of others. Whatever events occur, consider things solely in terms of how to make Buddhism flourish and how to bring benefit to all beings. There is a saying: 'Know before speaking, consider before acting.' Always be prudent. Consider the true meaning of whatever comes before you.

"Right before your eyes you can see that the moments pass without stopping, that the days flow in ever-changing progression, and that all is swiftly transient. Don't wait for the instruction of a teacher or for the *sūtra*s. Use each fleeting moment, and do not count on tomorrow. Think only of this day and this hour, for tomorrow is an uncertain thing; and no one knows what the future will bring. Make up your mind to follow Buddhism as if you had only this day to live. To follow Buddhism means, on all occasions and at the risk of your life, to make it flourish and bring benefit to all beings."

Someone asked: "Must one beg in order to promote Buddhism?"

Dōgen answered: "Yes, one must, but one must take into account the customs of the country. In any event, it must be done to spread benefit to all beings and to advance one's own training. If you wander about wearing a robe along dirty roads, the robe is bound to get dirty. Also, since the people in Japan are poor, it is impossible to beg in the prescribed manner.[44] But does this mean that we have to go backwards in our practice and limit the benefits we bring to others? If you just observe the customs of the country and practice Buddhism for all to see, people of all classes will of themselves make offerings. When this happens, you can continue your own practice and bring benefit to others at the same time. Even begging must be thoroughly thought about, taking into consideration the time and the circumstances.

Without concerning yourself with what people think and forgetting personal gain, you should just plan to do whatever you can to advance Buddhism and benefit all living beings."

21

Dōgen instructed:

Students, there is an important point to watch when you cast aside worldly concerns. You must give up the world you have known, your family, your body, and your mind. Consider this well.

Although they have escaped from the world and concealed themselves deep in mountain forests, there are some who cannot break with a family that has continued over many generations; nor can they keep from thinking of the members of their family and their relatives. There are others who have broken free from world, family, and the influence of relatives, yet concern themselves with their own bodies and avoid anything that brings pain. They are reluctant to undertake any Buddhist training that might endanger their health. Such people have yet to cast aside their bodies. Then there are those who undergo hard training without regard for their own bodies, yet withhold their minds from Buddhism. They reject any aspect of Buddhism that does not match their preconceptions. Such people have yet to cast aside their minds.

II

1
Dōgen instructed:

Practicers, if you just harmonize your minds at first, it will be easy to cast aside both your bodies and the world. If you worry about how others will react to your words and deportment, if you refrain from doing certain things because others will consider them bad, or if you do good thinking that others will admire you for it as a Buddhist, you still cling to the conditioned world. On the other hand, those who deliberately act with ill will are really bad men. Just forget evil intentions, forget your body, and act only for Buddhism. Be aware of each thing as it arises.

Those who are just starting out in Buddhism may discriminate and think in secular terms. Their attempt to refrain from evil and to practice good with their bodies constitutes casting aside both body and mind.

2
Dōgen instructed:

While the late Abbot Eisai was living at Kenninji, a poor man from the neighborhood came and said: "My home is so poor that my wife and I and our three children have had nothing to eat for several days. Have pity and help us out."

This was at a time when the monastery was completely without food, clothing, and money. Eisai racked his brains but could think of no solution. Then it occurred to him that just at this time a statue of Yakushi[1] was being built at the temple and that there was a bit of copper that had been hammered out to make the halo. Eisai broke it up with his own hands, made it into a ball, and gave it to the poor man. "Exchange this for

---

food and save your family from starvation," he said. The poor man left overjoyed.

His disciples were critical: "You've given the halo of a Buddhist statue to a layman. Isn't it a crime to make personal use of what belongs to the Buddha?"

"You are right," the Abbot replied, "but think of the will of the Buddha. He cut off his own flesh and limbs for the sake of all sentient beings. Certainly he would have sacrificed his entire body to save starving people. Even though I should fall into the evil realms for this crime, I will still have saved people from starvation." Students today would do well to reflect on the excellence of Eisai's attitude. Do not forget this.

On another occasion, his disciples remarked: "The buildings of the Kenninji are close to the river. In the future they may well be damaged by floods."

Eisai said: "Don't worry about what happens to our temple in years to come. After all, all that is left of the temple at Jetavana² are its stone foundations. This doesn't mean that the merit of establishing the temple has been lost. At any rate, the merit of practicing for six months or a year at the time that the Kenninji was being founded is certainly enormous.

As I think about this now, establishing a temple is one of the most important things a person can do in his life. It is only natural to wish that it will survive the future without damage. But the nobleness of purpose and profundity of Eisai must certainly be remembered.

3

In a talk one evening Dōgen said:

In China during the reign of Emperor T'ai-tsung³ of the T'ang, Wei Cheng⁴ remarked to the Emperor: "Your subjects are criticizing you."

The Emperor said: "If I am benevolent and draw criticism, I need not worry. But if I am not benevolent and am praised, then I should worry."

If even laymen have this attitude, how much more so should a monk. If you have compassion and a mind that seeks the Way, you need not concern yourself with the criticism of fools. If you don't have this mind, but people think you do, this is really a cause for concern.

On another occasion Dōgen instructed:

Emperor Wen-ti[5] of the Sui Dynasty once advised: "Pile up virtue in secret and wait for it to accumulate fully." What he way saying is to practice virtue thoroughly, wait for it to pile up fully, and then to guide people to rectitude. A monk who is not equal to this must be particularly careful. Virtue practiced inwardly manifests itself on the outside. If you just follow Buddhism and the Way of the Patriarchs without hoping for public recognition, the people will naturally seek refuge in Buddhist virtue. Many students make the mistake of thinking that virtue appears when people show them respect and make rich offerings. Others, seeing this, also come to the same conclusion. This sort of attitude is indeed the work of demons and must be guarded against with particular care. In the teachings, it is spoken of as the action of demons. I have yet to hear of any occasion in India, China, or Japan where a person has become virtuous by gaining riches and the respect of fools. From ancient times in these countries the true practicer of Buddhism has been poor, endured physical hardships, and wasted nothing. He has been motivated by compassion and the Way. Virtue is not expressed in abundant treasures and pride in the offerings received from others. Virtue shows itself in three stages: first, a person becomes known for practicing the Way; then, others so inclined come to him; and finally, they also study the Way and act in accord with it. This is called expressing virtue.

4

In an evening talk Dōgen said:

Students must cast aside worldly craving. To cast it aside is to practice according to Buddhism. Most people take the Hīnayāna attitude: discriminating between good and evil, and right and wrong, they accept the good and reject the evil. This is the Hīnayāna view. The first thing you must do, however, is to abandon secular views and to enter into the Buddha Way. To enter the Buddha Way is to stop discriminating between good and evil and to cast aside the mind that says this is good and that is bad. You must forget thoughts about what is good for your own body or what suits your own mind and follow the words and actions of the

Buddhas and Patriarchs, whether they seem good or bad.

What you in your own mind consider good or what people in the world think is good is by no means necessarily good. Therefore, forget what other people say, cast aside your own mind, and just follow the teachings of Buddhism. Even if you know that your body will suffer and your mind will be tormented and are convinced that you must completely forsake your body and mind, you must still follow what the Buddhas and Patriarchs have done. On the other hand, even though you want to do something that you think is good and accords with Buddhism, do not do so unless it agrees with the conduct of the Buddhas and Patriarchs. It is they who fully understand the Buddhist teachings.

Throw away ideas you have in your mind and concepts of the doctrine acquired in the past. Just turn your mind to the words and actions of the Zen Master that you see before you now. If you do this, your wisdom will increase, and enlightenment will unfold. You must think in terms of the meaning before you now and abandon any knowledge gained from the scriptural writings you have studied before, as well as any principles that need to be discarded. Study of the teachings is, from the outset, for the purpose of leaving the world and gaining the Way. Some of you probably wonder how merits acquired over many years of study can be given up so easily, but a mind such as this is still in bondage to the deluded world of birth and death. Think about this well.

5

In an evening talk Dōgen said:

The biography of Eisai, the late Abbot of Kenninji, was written by Akikane Chūnagon,[6] who became a Buddhist monk. At first, he declined the assignment, saying: "This biography should be written by a Confucian; a Confucian forgets his body and, from childhood to maturity, concentrates on study. There are no errors in what he writes. Ordinarily, people concentrate on their own work and social activities and engage in study as a sideline only. They may be talented writers, but they do make errors in their writing." It would seem that in olden days even people who studied non-Buddhist texts learned to forget the body.

The late Abbot Kōin[7] said: "The mind that seeks the Way is one that studies, takes to itself, and holds the teaching of the three thousand worlds in an instant of thought.[8] To tie a rain hood around one's neck and wander about in delusion is the conduct of someone seduced by the *tengu*."[9]

6

In a talk one evening Dōgen said:

The late Abbot Eisai always used to tell us: "Don't think that I'm the one who gives you the clothing and food that you use. These are all offered by the many devas. I only get them and pass them on to you. Each person receives an allotted portion during his life. Don't rush about looking for more, and don't feel obligated to me for them." These, I think, are the most splendid of words.

In the assembly at T'ien-t'ung of which Hung-chih[10] was Master, provisions were kept to provide for one thousand persons a day. Some seven hundred of these were practicing meditation, and three hundred worked in the temple compound. Because of Hung-chih's great reputation as a teacher, monks gathered from all over, until there were a thousand practicing monks and some five or six hundred engaged in temple work. Finally, one of the monks charged with administration appealed to Hung-chih: "We have provisions for only a thousand people, but so many have gathered here that we don't have sufficient supplies. Please send the extra people away."

Hung-chih replied: "Every one has a mouth to feed. It's not your worry, so don't complain."

When one thinks about it, everyone has his allotted share of food and clothing while he is alive. It does not come from thinking about it; nor does one fail to get it because one does not seek for it. Laymen leave such matters to fate, while they concern themselves with loyalty and develop their filial piety. How much less then should monks be governed by worldly concerns! Sākyamuni left the remaining portion of his life[11] to his descendants, and the many devas give food and clothing in offering. Each person naturally receives his allotted share in his life. He need not think of it, he need not search for it; the allotted portion is there. Even if you rush about in search of riches, what happens when death suddenly comes? Students should clear their minds of these non-essential things and concentrate on studying the Way.

Someone once said: "For Buddhism to flourish in this age, one must live in a quiet place where there is no need to worry about food and clothing. If one practices Buddhism with these necessities provided for, the benefits would be great." This does not strike me as true. If a group of people who are attached to form and the self gather together for study, there won't be one among them whose mind will be stirred to follow the Way. As long as they seek profit and gain, even if ten million people assembled together, there would not be a single one who would seek the Way. All they would do would be to accumulate the karma leading to the evil realms, and they would have no inclination for Buddhism.

But if someone comes to you and wants to study, after hearing that monks live in extreme austerity, subsist on begging, make do with fruits and grain, and practice hard even while hungry, then that person is a true seeker of the Way, and Buddhism will prosper. To have no one at all practicing amidst difficult and spotless poverty and to have many people assembled amidst an abundance of food and clothing, but without true Buddhism, is six of one thing and half a dozen of another.

On another occasion Dōgen said:

Many people today think that the making of statues and building of pagodas cause Buddhism to prosper. This, too, is not so. No one gained the Way by erecting lofty buildings that have gleaming jewels and gold adornments. This merely is a good action that gives blessings by bringing lay treasures into the Buddhist world. Although small causes can have large effects, Buddhism does not prosper if monks engage in such activities. If you learn one phrase of the Buddha's teaching or practice *zazen* even for a moment in a thatched hut or even under a tree, Buddhism will truly flourish.

I am now trying to build a monastery[12] and am asking people for contributions. While this requires much effort on my part, I cannot believe that it necessarily stimulates

Buddhism. It is just that nowadays there is no one who wants to study Buddhism, and I have much time on my hands. Since there is no place now for them to study, I want to provide a place for students to practice *zazen,* should any deluded followers appear who might wish to establish a connection with Buddhism. If my plans do not work out, I will have no regrets. If I can put up just one pillar, I won't care if people see it later and think that I had a plan but was unable to carry it out.

7

Once someone advised Dōgen to go to Eastern Japan if he wanted to see Buddhism prosper.

Dōgen said: "I don't agree. If anyone really wants to study Buddhism, he will come here, even if he has to cross mountains, rivers, and seas. If I take my teaching to people who do not have the desire to study, I don't know whether they will listen to me. Might I not just be leading people astray for the sake of my own livelihood or because I want material wealth? This would just wear me out. I can't see the point in going."

8

On another occasion Dōgen instructed:

Students of the Way should neither read the scriptures of other Buddhist teachings nor study non-Buddhist texts. If you do read, examine the writings of Zen. Other works should be put aside for a while.

Zen monks are fond of literature these days, finding it an aid to writing verses and tracts. This is a mistake. Even if you cannot compose verse, just write what is in your heart. Grammatical niceties do not matter if you just express the teachings of the Buddha. Those who lack the mind that seeks the Way may complain that someone's writing is bad. Yet no matter how elegant their prose or how exquisite their poetry might be, they are merely toying with words and cannot gain the Truth. I have loved literature since I was young and even now recall beautiful phrases from non-Buddhist works. I have been tempted to take up such books as the *Wen-hsüan,* but I have come to feel that it would be a waste of time and am inclined to think that such reading should be cast aside completely.

9

One day Dōgen instructed:

When I was at a Zen monastery in China reading the sayings of the old Zen Masters, a monk from Szechuan asked me: "What's the use of reading these Zen sayings?"

I replied: "To understand the actions of the old Masters."

The monk said: "What's the use of this?"

I replied: "I want to be able to guide people when I return to Japan."

The monk asked: "What's the use of that?"

"To benefit all beings," I said.

The monk then asked: "But what's the use in the long run?"

I thought about this later. Reading Zen sayings and *kōans* and understanding the actions of the Zen Masters of old to preach them to deluded people are all ultimately useless, either for one's own practice or for guiding others. If you clarify the Vital Principle in concentrated *zazen,* you have unlimited ways to guide others, even though you may not know a single word. This is why that monk spoke of "use in the long run." Accepting that his was the true principle, I later stopped reading the Zen sayings and other writings. I was thus able to gain awakening to the Vital Principle.

10

In a talk one evening Dōgen said:

You do not deserve the respect of others unless you have true virtue within yourself. Because the people of Japan respect others for their outward appearance, without knowing the true inner virtues, students without the mind that seeks the Way fall into evil paths and become the followers of demons. It is easy to be respected by others. One need merely give the impression of having forsaken the body and of being separated from the world by the external appearance one adopts. The true seeker of the Way harmonizes his mind and yet lives humbly like any other ordinary person in the world.

Therefore, an ancient sage has said: "Inwardly empty yourself, and outwardly follow the world." This means that you must rid yourself of inner attachments yet outwardly conform to the ways of the world. If you forget entirely your body and mind, enter into Buddhism, and practice according to the Buddhist teachings, you become good inwardly and outwardly both now and in the future.

Although Buddhism says to discard the body and abandon the world, it is wrong to cast aside things that should not be cast aside. In this country, among those who try to pass themselves off as Buddhists and seekers of the Way are some who say that, since they have forsaken their bodies, it does not matter what others think; and they act with unreasonable rudeness. Or else, saying that they are no longer attached to the world, they walk about heedlessly in the rain and get soaking wet. These actions serve no purpose either inwardly or outwardly, yet ordinary people have the impression that this type of person should be respected, because he seems to be detached from the world. On the other hand, the monk who upholds the Buddhist tenets, knows the precepts, and follows the Buddhist Way, in that he practices for himself and guides others, is likely to be ignored by people who feel that he is looking for fame and profit. To me the second type of monk is following the Buddhist teachings and has a better chance of developing both inner and outer virtues.

11

In a talk one evening Dōgen said:

Students, it is useless to be known by the world as a man of knowledge. If there is even one person who sincerely wants to learn Buddhism, you must not withhold from him whatever teachings of the Buddhas and the Patriarchs you possess. Even if he comes intending to kill you, if he should ask about the True Way with sincerity, forget your resentment and teach him. It is completely worthless to pretend to have a knowledge of the esoteric and exoteric teachings and to seem conversant with Buddhist and non-Buddhist works. If someone comes and asks about them, there is absolutely nothing wrong in saying that you don't know. It is a terrible mistake to study the scriptures of Buddhism and other teachings in an attempt to widen your knowledge either because others think it is bad not to know things or because you yourself feel stupid. Some even go as far as to study secular affairs in order to give the impression that they have a love of learning. For studying the Way, these things are of no use whatsoever. Yet to know and pretend you don't is unnatural and creates a bad impression. It is best not to know from the beginning.

When I was young, I enjoyed studying ordinary books. Later I went to China, and until the time I returned to Japan, I read both Buddhist and lay works and even became proficient in the native dialect. Because of various duties and my associations with the secular world, I gained a knowledge of a great variety of things. As I look back on it now, all this was a hindrance to my practice, although I did learn many things that laymen find difficult. While reading the sacred scriptures, one can gradually come to understand the Buddhist truth as it is revealed in the text. It is a mistake, though, to first look at the sentences, to concern oneself with the alignment of phrases and their rhymes, to evaluate them as good or bad, and then try to grasp the truth. Instead, it is better to disregard literary considerations and to grasp the truth of the text from the outset. In writing popular sermons and other works, if you attempt to compose good sentences and to avoid infelicities in rhyme, you err because of the knowledge you have. You should steadily set down the truth as it comes to mind, without regard to vocabulary and style. Even though the sentences may seem ragged afterwards, you contribute to Buddhism if the truth is there. This applies to other studies as well.

There is a story about the late Kū Amidabutsu of Mount Kōya.[13] He was originally a famous scholar of exoteric and esoteric Buddhism. After abandoning the world, he turned to the study of *Nembutsu*.[14] When later a Shingon priest came to ask him about the teachings of esoteric Buddhism, he replied: "I have forgotten everything. I don't remember a single word."

This is a good example of the mind that seeks the Way. With such a background, he certainly should have remembered something. But what he said is much to the point, for from the day he entered into the *Nembutsu* teachings, such an attitude was appropriate. Zen students today must have the same attitude. Even though they may know the scriptures of other teachings, they must forget them all; not only that, but they must not consider even for an instant about learning them now. The true practicing Zen monk should not even read the *Records* of the old Masters and other writings. This applies to other works as well.

12

In a talk one evening Dōgen said:

In this country today, many students worry about the good and evil, and right and wrong, of their own speech and actions and wonder how others will react to what they see and hear. They are concerned about whether something they do will draw censure or bring praise now or in the future. This is a very bad state of affairs. What the world considers good is not necessarily good. It does not matter what other people think; let them call you a madman. If you spend your life with your mind in harmony with Buddhism and do nothing to offend against it, the views of other people do not matter in the least.

To escape from the world means that one's mind is not concerned with the opinions of the world. Just study and practice the actions of the Buddhas and the Patriarchs and the compassion of the Bodhisattvas, reflect on yourself as if heavenly deities were illuminating your faults, and act in accord with the Buddhist rules; then nothing will trouble you.

On the other hand, it is an error to blithely ignore what others consider bad and arbitrarily do evil things in complete disregard of the criticism of others. Without concerning yourself with what others think, act only in accordance with Buddhism. In Buddhism arbitrary actions and shameless conduct are forbidden.

13

On another occasion Dōgen said:

Even by the standards of ordinary society, lack of propriety—such as changing your clothing improperly, even when you are where people cannot see you or are in a darkened room; or sitting or lying indecently so that parts that should be hidden are exposed—is an insult to heaven and to ghosts. Hide what should be hidden, and be ashamed of what is shameful, just as if you were always in the presence of others. This reflects the intent of the precepts. Those versed in the Way must not make distinctions about whether they are inside a room or outside it, or whether it is light or dark, and do bad things just because they are out of sight of people who know the Buddhist regulations.

14

One day a student asked: "I have spent months and years in earnest study, but I have yet to gain enlightenment. Many of the old Masters say that the Way does not depend on intelligence and cleverness and that there is no need for knowledge and talent. As I understand it, even though my capacity is inferior, I need not feel badly of myself. Are there any old sayings or cautionary words that I should know about?"

Dōgen replied: "Yes, there are. True study of the Way does not rely on knowledge and genius or cleverness and brilliance. But it is a mistake to encourage people to be like blind men, deaf mutes, or imbeciles. Because study has no use for wide learning and high intelligence, even those with inferior capacities can participate. True study of the Way is an easy thing.

But even in the monasteries of China, only one or two out of several hundred, or even a thousand, disciples under a great Zen Master actually gained true enlightenment. Therefore, old sayings and cautionary words are needed. As I see it now, it is a matter of gaining the desire to practice. A person who gives rise to a real desire and puts his utmost efforts into study under a teacher will surely gain enlightenment. Essentially, one must devote all attention to this effort and enter into practice with all due speed. More specifically, the following points must be kept in mind:

"In the first place, there must be a keen and sincere desire to seek the Way. For example, someone who wishes to steal a precious jewel, to attack a formidable enemy, or to make the acquaintance of a beautiful woman must, at all times, watch intently for the opportunity, adjusting to changing events and shifting circumstances. Anything sought for with such intensity will surely be gained. If the desire to search for the Way becomes as intense as this, whether you concentrate on doing *zazen* alone, investigate a *kōan* by an old Master, interview a Zen teacher, or practice with sincere devotion, you will succeed no matter how high you must shoot or no matter how deep you must plumb. Without arousing this wholehearted will for the Buddha Way, how can anyone succeed in this most important task of cutting the endless round of birth and death? Those who have this drive, even if they have little knowledge or are of inferior capacity, even if they are stupid or evil, will without fail gain enlightenment.

"Next, to arouse such a mind, one must be deeply aware of the impermanence of the world. This realization is not achieved by some temporary method of contemplation. It is not creating something out of nothing and then thinking about it. Impermanence is a fact before our eyes. Do not wait for the teachings from others, the words of the scriptures, and for the principles of enlightenment. We are born in the morning and die in the evening; the man we saw yesterday is no longer with us today. These are facts we see with our own eyes and hear with our own ears. You see and hear impermanence in terms of another person, but try weighing it with your own body. Even though you live to be seventy or eighty, you die in accordance with the inevitability of death. How will you ever come to terms with the worries, joys, intimacies, and conflicts that concern you in this life? With faith in Buddhism, seek the true happiness of Nirvana. How can those who are old or who have passed the halfway mark in their lives relax in their studies when there is no way of telling how many years are left?

"Even this is putting it too simply. Think of what might happen today, this very moment, in the ordinary world and the Buddhist world as well. Perhaps tonight, perhaps tomorrow, you will fall seriously ill; find your body racked with unendurable pain; die suddenly, cursed by some unknown demons; meet misfortune at the hands of robbers; or be slain by someone seeking vengeance. Life is indeed an uncertain thing. In this hateful world where death may come at any moment, it is absurd to plan your life, intrigue maliciously against others, and spend your time in fruitless pursuits.

"Because impermanence is a fact of life, the Buddha spoke of it for the sake of all beings, and the Patriarchs preached of this alone. Even now in the lecture hall and in their instructions, Zen Masters dwell on the swiftness of impermanence and the vital matter of birth and death. I repeat, don't forget this truth. Think only of this very moment, and waste no time in turning your minds to the study of the Way. After this it is easy. It has nothing to do with the quality of your nature or the dullness or keenness of your capacity."

15
In a talk one evening Dōgen said:

Many people do not escape from this world because, while seeming to treasure the body, they actually do not give it adequate consideration. Their thinking is not deep enough because they have yet to meet a good teacher. Considered in terms of profit, they stand to gain the blessings of unlimited joy and may seek offerings from dragons and devas. Looked at in terms of fame, they have a chance to gain the respect of future sages by attaining to the renown of the Buddhas and Patriarchs and the ancient men of virtue.

16
In a talk one evening Dōgen said:

According to Confucius, one should: "In the morning hear the Way, in the evening die content." Students today should emulate this attitude. Over long eons we have on innumerable occasions gone through the process of being born and dying, yet rarely have we had the chance of obtaining a human body and becoming acquainted with Buddhism. If we do not save ourselves now, in what world can we expect to do so? It is impossible to retain this body no matter how we treasure it. Since in the end we all must die, if we dedicate our bodies to Buddhism for a day or even for a moment, we lay the basis for eternal peace.

It is a sorry thing to spend your days and nights in vain, thinking about things that might be, planning for tomorrow's livelihood, and hesitating to forsake what should be forsaken and to practice what should be practiced. At the outset, arouse the determination to hear the Way and follow the Buddha mind for just this one day, even if you should die. What if you starve or freeze to death because you have no means of livelihood tomorrow? If you do this, you will not err in practicing and gaining the Way.

Those who cannot rouse this determination, even though they seem to have escaped from the world to study the Way, worry about their clothing in summer and winter and about what means of livelihood they will have tomorrow or the next year. Those who approach Buddhism in this manner will not be able to understand it, even if they study for endless kalpas. There are indeed people like this, but this certainly does not represent the teachings of the Buddhas and the Patriarchs that I know.

17

In a talk one evening Dōgen said:

Students must thoroughly consider the fact that they will eventually die. While you may not think about death directly, you must make sure not to waste time. Instead of spending time fruitlessly, use it for meaningful activities. If you wonder what the most important of all things is, it is to know the way in which the Buddhas and the Patriarchs conducted themselves. All else is of no use whatsoever.

18

Once Ejō asked: "If a Zen monk refuses to throw away an old, mended robe, it looks as though he is coveting it. If he throws away an old robe and acquires a new one, he seems to be attached to the new. Both views are wrong. What attitude should one take?"

Dōgen answered: "If you can free yourself from both covetousness and attachment, neither will be wrong. Wouldn't it be better, though, to mend a torn robe and use it for a long time rather than long for a new one?"

19

Following an evening talk, Ejō asked: "Must we fulfill our obligations to our parents?"

Dōgen instructed: "Filial piety is most important, but there is a difference between laymen and monks. Laymen, relying on such works as the *Book of Filial Piety*, take care of their parents during their lifetimes and hold services for them after their deaths. Monks, on the other hand, have severed their ties with the world and live in the religious realm. Thus their obligations are not limited to parents alone, but, feeling these obligations to all beings, they fill the world with good deeds. If they were merely to limit their obligations to their parents, they would be turning against the religious way. True filial piety consists in following Buddhism in everyday practice and in each moment of study under a Zen Master. Offering services on the anniversary of a parent's death and doing good for forty-nine days[15] belong to the activities of the lay world. Zen monks must understand the deep obligations they bear their parents in the above terms. So must they in the same way know all other obligations. Does selecting just one day for doing good and holding services[16] for just one person really reflect the spirit of Buddhism? Is the passage in the *Precept Sutra,* which deals with the day when parents and brothers die, primarily for laymen? In the monasteries of China, monks hold a ceremony upon the anniversary of the death of the Zen Master but do not seem to do so on the date of their parents' death."

20

One day Dōgen instructed:

If you talk about a person's cleverness or stupidity, it shows that you have yet to arouse the determination to study Buddhism. When an ordinary person falls off a horse, many things rush through his mind before he even hits the ground. In the same way, when any great threat to life and limb occurs, everybody devotes his full thought and knowledge in an effort to escape from harm. At such times, nobody, whether he be clever or stupid, thinks any differently from anybody else. Therefore, if you can spur and arouse your determination with the thought that you might die tonight or tomorrow or that at any time you might meet with some terrible misfortune, you can expect to gain enlightenment. A dull person, if he earnestly gives rise to the determination, will gain enlightenment faster than someone who is merely intelligent and eloquent. During the Buddha's lifetime, Kṣudrapanthaka[17] had trouble reading even a single line of verse, yet since he sought the Way intently, he gained enlightenment during one period of retreat. You are alive only right now. Anyone can gain enlightenment if he studies Buddhism earnestly, vowing that he must awaken before death cuts off his fleeting life.

21
In a talk one evening Dōgen said:

At a Zen monastery in China, the monks were in the habit of sorting the wheat and rice, separating the good from the bad and making their meals from the good alone.

A Zen Master warned against this practice in verse: "Even if my head were split into seven pieces, I would not sort the rice." What he meant was that monks should not concern themselves with what they have to eat. Just take what is there. If it is good, enjoy it; if it is bad, eat it without distaste. Just practice, eating enough to avoid starving, and maintain your life with the food provided by the faithful donors and with the unstained food stored in the monastery. This means that you are not to pass judgment on the food on the basis of how it tastes. You students studying under me now should bear this in mind.

22
Once someone asked: "Supposing a student, hearing it taught that he himself is the Buddhadharma and that one must not seek it outside, should acquire great faith in these words, abandon the practice, study under a teacher that had occupied him until then, and spend his life, doing both good and bad in accordance with his own inclinations. What would you think of this?"

Dōgen instructed: "This view fails to match the words with their meaning. To say, 'Do not seek the Buddhadharma outside,' and then to cast aside practice and study, implies that one is seeking by the very act of casting aside. This is not true to the fact that practice and study are both inherently the Buddhadharma. If, without seeking anything, you detach yourself from worldly affairs and evil actions, even though they may attract you; if, even though you may not feel like practice and study, you carry it out anyway; if you practice wholeheartedly with this attitude and still gain the good rewards—then the very fact that you have practiced seeking nothing for yourself accords with the principle of 'not seeking the Buddhadharma on the outside.'

"When Nan-yüeh[18] made his remark about not trying to polish a piece of tile to make a mirror, he was warning his disciple Ma-tsu[19] against striving to become a Buddha by practicing *zazen*. He was not trying to proscribe *zazen* itself. *Zazen* is the practice of the Buddha. *Zazen* is the ultimate practice. This is indeed the True Self. The Buddhadharma is not to be sought outside of this."

23

One day Dōgen gave the following reply to a question from a disciple:

Many monks these days say that they must follow the ways of the world. This I do not believe. Even among laymen the wise know that, if one follows the ways of the world, one is defiled by them. For example, Ch'ü Yüan[20] said: "Everybody in the world is drunk. Only I am sober!" He refused to follow the ways of the world until he ended his life in the waters of the Ts'ang-lang River.

Buddhism differs completely from the usual ways of the world. Ordinary people adorn their hair; monks shave it off. Ordinary people eat several times a day; monks, just once. They differ in everything. Yet later the monks become men who have gained the great tranquility. For monks, then, the ways of the world should be shunned.

24

One day Dōgen instructed:

The laws that control the world provide that each person, from Emperor to commoner, does the work that his position demands. When a person occupies a position he is not qualified to hold, it is known as disturbing the Will of Heaven. When the government accords with the Will of Heaven, the world is calm and the people at peace. Thus the Emperor arises early[21] in the morning to perform his duties; this is not easy work. The laws of the Buddha differ only so far as the occupation and type of work is concerned. When the Emperor governs on the basis of his own thinking, takes into account the precedents of the past, and seeks out virtuous ministers and when his government accords with the Will of Heaven, then good government prevails throughout the land. When these things are neglected, there is conflict with heaven, disturbances fill the world, and the common people suffer. From the Emperor on down—all officials, functionaries, warriors, and commoners—have the particular work that they must do. Those who follow their calling are true men. Because those who do not perform their duties disturb the affairs of heaven, they receive its punishment.

Therefore, students of Buddhism, in that they abandon both the world and their homes, must not think of bodily comfort even for a moment. Although this comfort may seem useful at first, later it can cause only great harm. Monks must train themselves to perform their duties fully and to do their work in the way expected. Governing a country requires an understanding of past rules and laws, but, when no examples have been transmitted from the former sages and wise men, one must follow what seems the proper thing to do at the time. The Buddhist, however, has clear precedents and teachings to follow. Masters who have received the teachings handed down directly from the past are living today.

Once you realize that for each of the four dignified attitudes[22] there are established precedents and that you must just practice in the manner of your predecessors, then you cannot help but gain the Way. Ordinary people think of conforming to the Will of Heaven; Zen monks think of conforming to the will of the Buddha. While each must approach his labors in the same way, what is gained differs, for the monk gains something far better, something that once attained lasts forever. For the sake of this great tranquility, the practicer must only determine in his own heart to undergo the temporary hardships that befall this illusory body during one lifetime and to follow the will of the Buddha.

Yet Buddhism does not teach that your body must suffer pain or that you must do the impossible. If you observe the rules and precepts, your body naturally feels at ease, your actions take on grace, and your appearance attracts others. Consider this and abandon the egoistic view of bodily tranquility you now hold and follow wholeheartedly the regulations of Buddhism.

25

On another occasion Dōgen said:

When I stayed at the T'ien-t'ung monastery in China, the Abbot Ju-ching practiced *zazen* until about eleven o'clock at night, then got up at two-thirty or three, and started in again. He sat in the meditation hall with the elder monks, without missing a single night. In the meantime, many of the other monks in the assembly would fall asleep. Ju-ching made the rounds striking the sleeping monks with his fist or slipper, shaming them and demanding that they wake up. If some of the monks still persisted in sleeping, he would go to the small building to the rear of the meditation hall, strike a bell, and summon an attendant. By candlelight, he would deliver a lecture to the whole assembly.

"What's the use of gathering in the meditation hall and then wasting your time sleeping? Is this what you left your homes and entered the monastery for? Do you see the Emperor, government officials, or anybody, for that matter, living a life of ease? The Emperor has to carry out the functions of a ruler, the ministers must serve with loyalty, commoners must clear land and till the soil; who can spend his time in a life of ease? What's the point of leaving the ordinary world and entering a Zen monastery if your are only going to waste time? Birth and death are vital matters; intransiency is always upon us. Zen and the teaching schools all agree in this. Death or some dread disease may strike tonight or tomorrow morning. With time so short, how foolish it is to fail to practice the Buddhadharma and to waste one's time in sleep. This is what makes the Law of the Buddha decline. When Buddhism flourished everywhere, monks in all Zen monasteries concentrated solely on *zazen*. Because *zazen* is not vigorously encouraged these days, Buddhism is declining."

With these words, the Master encouraged his followers to practice *zazen*. This is something I saw with my own eyes. Students today should give careful thought to this style of Zen.

On another occasion, an attendant said to Ju-ching: "Some of the monks here are exhausted from lack of sleep, some are ill, and others have lost their desire to seek the Way. Perhaps the meditation periods are too long and should be shortened."

The Master was infuriated: "Absolutely not. Those who don't have the mind that seeks the Way would fall asleep in the meditation hall even if the sitting period were shortened. For those who practice with determination, the longer the sitting period, the more they enjoy their sitting. When I was young, I used to visit Zen Masters all over the country. One of them once told me:[23] 'If a monk was sleeping, I used to strike him until my fist almost broke. But now, I have grown old and weak and cannot hit so hard. That is why good monks are hard to produce. Because Zen Masters everywhere have an easy-going attitude towards *zazen,* Buddhism is declining. We must begin again to hit them harder.' "

26
On another occasion Dōgen said:

Is the Way attained through the mind or through the body? The teaching schools say that, since body and mind are identical, it is attained through the body. Yet since they say that body and mind are identical, it is not explicitly stated that the Way is attained by the body. In Zen the Way is attained with both body and mind. If you contemplate Buddhism with the mind alone, not for ten thousand kalpas or a thousand lives can you attain the Way. But if you let go the mind and cast aside knowledge and intellectual understanding, you will gain the Way. Those who gained enlightenment by seeing blossoms or hearing sounds[24] achieved it through the body. Therefore, if you cast aside completely the thoughts and concepts of the mind and concentrate on *zazen* alone, you attain to an intimacy with the Way. The attainment of the Way is truly accomplished with the body. For this reason, I urge you to concentrate on *zazen.*

III

1

Dōgen instructed:

Students, cast aside your bodies and minds and enter fully into Buddhism.

An old Master has said: "You've climbed to the top of a hundred-foot pole. Now keep on going."[1] Most people, when they reach the top, are afraid they will lose their footing and fall to their deaths. Thus they hang on all the more tightly. To advance another step means to discard all thoughts of everything, from your functions as a savior of other beings to the means of your own livelihood, even if it requires casting away your own life. If you do not do this and even if you study the Way as earnestly as though you were trying to put out flames in your own hair, you will not be able to attain the Way. Resolve to cast aside both body and mind.

2

A nun once asked Dōgen: "Even ordinary women engage in the study of Buddhism. Is there any reason then why a nun, despite the few small faults she may have, should be unfit for Buddhism?"

Dōgen replied: "You are wrong. Although ordinary women can study Buddhism and gain enlightenment as members of the lay community, those who have left their homes cannot gain the Way unless they have attained the necessary determination. It is not that Buddhism discriminates between people but that people do not enter into Buddhism. Monks and laymen have different motivations. A layman who thinks like a monk can free himself from delusion, but a monk who thinks like a layman compounds his error. The two approaches differ. It is not the doing that is difficult, but rather the doing it well that is hard. The practice of leaving the world and gaining the Way attracts many people, but there are few who do it well. Birth and death are vital matters; the changes of transiency are swift. Don't relax in your determination. If you are forsaking the world, then really forsake it. Provisional designations, such as layman or priest, seem of little significance.

3

In a talk one evening Dōgen said:

In looking at the world, I notice that the people who are richly rewarded and bring prosperity to their homes are those with consideration for others. They maintain comfortable homes, and their descendants prosper. Those with warped minds and ill feeling towards others usually meet misfortune, even though for a while they may seem to be well-rewarded and in comfortable circumstances. They may prosper for a while, but their descendants will without fail decline.

To do good for others in anticipation of their gratitude and happiness would appear to be better than doing evil, but this is not true goodness because you are still thinking of your own self. The truly good man does things for others, even if now or in the future they are in no way aware of it. How much better must the attitude of the Zen monk be! In considering people, do not differentiate between the intimate and the distant. Resolve to help all equally. Determine in your mind to benefit others, whether lay or clerical, without self-interest or profit, and without caring whether people know or appreciate your actions. Furthermore, do not let others know that you are acting from this standpoint.

From the outset, the essential has always been to abandon the world and cast aside your body. If you can truly discard your own body, the mind that seeks the appreciation of others disappears. On the other hand, if you don't care what people think, practice evil, and behave arbitrarily, you violate the will of the Buddha. Just practice good, do good for others, without thinking of making yourself known so that you may gain reward. Really bring benefit to others, gaining nothing for yourself. This is the primary requisite for breaking free of attachments to the Self.

To establish such an attitude, you must first understand impermanence. Our life is like a dream, and time passes swiftly. This dewlike existence easily fades away. Because time waits for no one, you should, during this short lifetime, vow to follow the Buddha's will and help others in every way possible, no matter how small.

4

In a talk one evening Dōgen said:

Students of the Way should be the poorest of all. One notices that people in this world who have wealth are inevitably plagued by two difficulties, anger and shame. If a person is rich, others try to rob him; and when he tries to prevent this, he suddenly gets angry. Or else a dispute arises, and there is a legal confrontation, which inevitably involves conflict. From such events, anger and shame arise. A person who is poor and without greed, however, will avoid such difficulty from the start and will be free and at ease. You can see the proof of this right before your eyes. You do not have to wait for textual confirmation, for even the sages and the wise men of the past condemned anger and shame, as did the devas, the Buddhas, and the Patriarchs. Yet the foolish accumulate wealth and nurse anger. This is a shame among shames. One who is poor and concentrates on the Way has the respect of the old sages and the men of wisdom and brings joy to the Buddhas and the Patriarchs.

Nowadays, the decline of Buddhism is evident. What I saw when I first entered the Kenninji was quite different from what I saw seven or eight years later. A gradual change had taken place. Now the dormitories have plaster-walled closets. Each monk has his own utensils, fine clothing, and other treasures. The monks like idle chatter, and the formal greetings and salutations are neglected. I assume that the same conditions prevail at other temples. Monks should have no possessions other than their robes and bowl. What are the plaster-walled closets for? There is no need for anything that has to be hidden from others. The more things stored, the greater is the fear of robbers. With no possessions, monks would be much more at ease. When one worries about killing someone and at the same time not being killed himself, he is tense and on guard. But someone who has no desire for revenge, even if he should be killed, finds no need for caution and has no need to worry about robbers. There is no time when he is not at ease.

5

One day Dōgen instructed:

When the Zen Master Hai-wen[2] was abbot of the monastery at Mt. T'ien-t'ung, there was a monk by the name of Yüan[3] in his assembly. Yüan was an enlightened man, and his attainments transcended even those of the Abbot.

One night he entered the Abbot's room, burned incense, made his obeisances, and said: "Please make me the supervisor of the monks in the rear meditation hall."[4]

With tears in his eyes, the Zen Master said: "From the day I entered this temple as a young monk until now, this is the first time I have ever heard a request of this sort. It is a serious mistake for a Zen monk like you to seek the position of supervisor or abbot. Your enlightenment already exceeds my own. Are you trying to advance yourself by seeking this position? If I were to agree to this, I might as well let you become supervisor of the front hall or even abbot. Your attitude is despicable. If even you are like this, I can just imagine what the attitude of the other monks who have yet to gain enlightenment must be. It certainly shows how far Buddhism has declined." Yüan withdrew in shame, but later he was appointed to be supervisor. Afterwards he recorded what the Master had said and made public his own shame in the fine words of the Master.

When one considers this, it is clear how the old Masters looked down on those who sought advancement, wanted to be in charge of things, or aimed at becoming abbot. Just concentrate on awakening to the Way and on nothing else.

6

During a talk one evening Dōgen said:

When Emperor T'ai-tsung of the T'ang Dynasty ascended the throne, he lived in the old palace buildings. The palace was damp and badly in need of repair, and wind and fog chilled the Emperor's body. When his ministers proposed that he build a new palace, the Emperor said: "It is now the harvest season. The people would be greatly inconvenienced. Let's wait to build until the season is over. Dampness plagues us because we do not accept the earth; wind and rain attack us because we do not harmonize with heaven. If we go against heaven and earth, we won't be able to preserve our bodies. If we do not bring trouble to the people, we will naturally be in harmony with heaven and earth. If we are in harmony with heaven and earth, our bodies will not be harmed." He finally decided not to build a new palace and continued to live in the old one.

When even a layman feels this way about the people, he has transcended his own body. How much more compassionate should the disciples of the Buddha, who follow in the style of the Tathāgata, be! Their compassion for all the people should be like that towards an only son. Don't scold and make trouble for your attendants and followers merely because they serve you. The precepts clearly state that you must respect your fellow students and the elder priests as you would the Tathāgata.

Therefore, students today should, without showing it, devote themselves to the good of others, without distinguishing between high and low, intimate or distant. Don't trouble others or hurt their feelings over matters, either trivial or important. While the Tathāgata was alive, there were many who scorned him as a heretic and hated him. A disciple once asked him: "You are by nature gentle and compassionate, and all beings venerate you equally. Why are there some who do not follow you?"

The Buddha replied: "In a former life, when I had charge of an assembly, I cautioned my disciples in a loud and scolding manner. In retribution things are what they are today." This story appears in a Vinaya text.

Therefore, even though you may have charge of an assembly as an abbot or senior priest, you must not use scolding words when you admonish your disciples and correct their errors. They will follow what should be followed if you admonish and encourage with gentle words. By all means stop using harsh words to scold others, whether they be students of the Way, relatives, or anyone else. Think this over well.

7

On another occasion Dōgen said:

Monks should take care to follow the conduct of the Buddha and the Patriarchs. Above all, do not covet wealth. It is impossible to put into words the depth of the Tathāgata's compassion. Everything he did was for the sake of all sentient beings. There was nothing that he did, no matter how small, that was not done for others. The Buddha was the son of a king and might have ascended the throne, had he so wished. Had he wanted, he could have bestowed treasures on his followers and furnished them with land. Why then did he give up his claims to the throne and become a beggar? It was to benefit people in the ages when the Law had declined and to encourage the practice of the Way that he set an example, by refusing to accumulate wealth and by becoming a beggar himself. Ever since, all the Patriarchs of India and China and all those who were known to the world as fine Buddhists have been poor and begged for their food. In our school all the Masters warn against the accumulation of wealth. When other sects speak well of Zen, the first thing that they praise is its poverty. In works that record the transmission, poverty is frequently mentioned and highly praised. I have yet to hear of a wealthy person who is engaged in the practice of Buddhism. Those who are recognized as good Buddhists wear coarse robes and beg. The fine reputation of Zen and the unique standing of its monks stem from the early days when they still lived in the temples of the Vinaya and other sects. From this early time Zen monks renounced their bodies and lived in poverty. This is recognized as an outstanding characteristic of the Zen school. Do not wait for the teachings and principles of the sacred scriptures. There was a time when I owned private lands and possessed wealth, but when I compare the state of my body and mind at that time to the way it is now, with only my robes and bowl, I realize how superior my present state is. In this lies the proof.

8

On another occasion Dōgen said:

A man of old has said: "Don't talk about the conduct of others if you don't resemble them." This means that, without knowing or studying a person's virtues, one should not, upon seeing his weaknesses, conclude that he is a good person but suffers certain defects and does bad things. Look just at his virtues, not his shortcomings. This is the meaning of the saying: "A superior man sees the virtues but not the shortcomings of others."

9
One day Dōgen instructed:

A person should always practice hidden virtue. If he does so, he will gain the benefits of unseen blessings. Even though it may be a crude statue made of sticks and mud, as an image of the Buddha, reverence it. Even though it may be a poorly written scroll with yellow paper and red holders, as a sacred scripture, venerate it. Even though a monk breaks the precepts and knows no shame, respect him as a member of the *sangha.* If you pay him respect with a believing mind, blessings will without fail appear. If the precept-breaking, the shameless monk, the crude image of the Buddha, and the shoddy scripture cause you to lose faith and withhold respect, you will without fail be punished. In the laws left behind by the Tathāgata, we find that Buddhist images, the sacred texts, and the priesthood bring blessings to men and devas. Therefore, if you venerate them, benefits will always accrue. If you have no faith in them, you will be punished. No matter how absurdly crude it may be, anything in the form of the Three Treasures must be respected. It is a grave error for Zen monks to prefer evil acts, saying that there is no need to practice good or to accumulate merits. I have never heard of any preference for evil acts in the Zen traditions of the past.

The Zen Master Tan-hsia T'ien-jan[5] burned a wooden image of the Buddha. Although this appears to be an evil act, it was meant to emphasize a point in his teaching. From the records of his life we learn that he always observed the proprieties, whether sitting or standing; when a guest was present, he always made sure to face him. Whenever he sat down, if only for a little while, he always assumed the full lotus position; when he stood, he held his hands folded lightly on his chest. He cared for the communal property of the monastery with utmost respect and was always ready with praise for a diligent monk. He esteemed highly even the slightest good, and his daily conduct was truly fine. A description of his life remains and, to this day, serves as a model for Zen monasteries. Furthermore, from what I have seen and heard, all the other enlightened Masters and the Patriarchs who attained the Way observed the precepts and the proprieties and esteemed highly even the slightest good. I have never heard of an enlightened Zen Master who made light of good capacities.

Therefore, students who aspire to follow the Patriarchal Way should never take good capacities lightly. Above all they must have complete faith in the Buddha's teaching. Where the Way of the Buddhas and Patriarchs is practiced, there all kinds of good accumulate. Once we have thoroughly realized that all things are the Buddhadharma, then we know that evil is always evil and is far from the Way of the Buddha and the Patriarchs and that good is always good, and is linked with the Buddha Way. If this is so, how can we not render homage to anything representative of the realm of the Three Treasures?

10
On another occasion Dōgen said:

If you wish to practice the Way of the Buddhas and the Patriarchs, you should follow without thought of profit the Way of the former sages and the conduct of the Patriarchs, expecting nothing, seeking nothing, and gaining nothing. Cut off the mind that seeks and do not cherish a desire to gain the fruits of Buddhahood. If you stop your practice and remain obsessed with your former evil actions, you fall prey even more strongly to the seeking mind and cannot climb out of the hole into which you have fallen.[6] If you expect nothing whatsoever and try only to bring benefit to men and devas, conduct yourself with the dignity of a monk, concern yourself with saving and benefitting others, practice various forms of good, discard the evil actions of the past, and do not rest content with the present good but continue your practice throughout your life; then you will be, in the words of the old Masters, one who has "broken the lacquered bucket."[7] This is what we call the conduct of the Buddhas and the Patriarchs.

11

One day a monk came up and asked about the essentials of the Way. Dōgen instructed: "Students must first of all be poor. If they have much wealth, they will certainly lose the desire for study. Those among the laity who study the Way, if they concern themselves with wealth and are attached to their dwellings and maintain close contact with their relatives, will find many obstructions to gaining the Way, even though they say that they have the determination to study. Since ancient times, many laymen have undertaken study under a Zen Master, but even the best of them rarely equaled the monks. Monks have no possessions other than their robes and bowl. They do not care where they live; they do not crave for clothing and food, but, concentrating on the study of the Way, each benefits according to his capacity. For this reason, the poverty of the monks is highly compatible with the Buddha Way.

"P'ang,[8] although a layman, was not inferior to the monks. His name is remembered in Zen because, when he first began to study under a Master, he took all the possessions from his house with the aim of throwing them into the sea. Someone advised him: 'You should give them to the people or use them for the cause of Buddhism.'

"P'ang replied: 'I'm throwing them away because I consider them an enemy. How can I give such things to others! Wealth is an adversary that brings only grief to body and mind.' In the end, he threw his treasures into the sea and afterwards earned his living by making and selling baskets. Though a layman, he is known as a good man because he discarded his wealth in this way. How much more necessary is it then for a monk to discard his treasures!"

12

A monk said: "In China the temples where Zen monks stayed were fixed, and provisions for the temple monks, as well as those for other monks who might chance to visit, were set aside. These provisions provided for the maintenance of practicing monks so that they did not have to worry about their livelihood. In this country, however, there is no such

---

custom, and, if we cast aside completely all our belongings, it serves to disrupt the practice of the Way. It would seem a good idea if our clothing and food could be provided for. What do you think?"

Dōgen said: "This is not so. People in this country give more wholehearted support to their monks than the Chinese do to theirs. Sometimes they even give beyond their means. I don't know about others, but I myself have had experience in this respect and know what I am talking about. Without depending on a single thing or even thinking of obtaining anything, I have managed to survive for more than ten years. Problems arise when one starts to think about accumulating possessions. During this brief life span of ours, even if we do not consider accumulating things, we will find that they are supplied naturally. Each person receives his allotted share, bestowed by heaven and earth. It is there even if we don't rush about in search of it. The disciples of the Buddha have a share of the legacy left by the Tathāgata and, in the course of things, obtain without seeking. If we cast aside our possessions and practice the Way with utmost effort, these things are naturally ours. The proof is before your very eyes."

13
On another occasion Dōgen said:

Students of the Way often ask: "If we do this, won't people criticize us?" This is a grave mistake. No matter how people may criticize, if your actions are in accord with the conduct of the Buddhas, the Patriarchs, and the principles of the sacred teachings, you should continue with them. Similarly, even though people praise your actions, if they do not conform to the principles of the sacred teachings and if they conflict with the practice of the Patriarchs, you should not go through with them.

If you base your actions on the praise and censure of friends or strangers, when you die and fall into the evil realms because of your own wrong doings, these people will not be able to save you. Even though you are criticized and hated by people, if you practice the Way of the Buddhas and the Patriarchs, you will truly be saved. Don't stop practicing the

Way just because you are criticized by others. People who criticize and praise in this manner have never penetrated to the conduct of the Buddhas and the Patriarchs; nor have they gained enlightenment. How can you judge the Way of the Buddhas and the Patriarchs on the basis of worldly standards of good and evil? Therefore, do not be moved by the emotions of other people. Just concentrate on following and practicing the truth of Buddhism.

14

On another occasion a monk said: "I am an only child, and my aged mother is still alive. She lives on what I am able to send her. We are deeply attached to each other, and my filial loyalties are strong. So, by compromising slightly with the world and its people, I can provide food and clothing for my mother through the support of others. If I were to renounce the world and live alone, my mother would have difficulty living even for one day. Thus, while participating in the ordinary world, I am distressed that I cannot enter wholeheartedly into Buddhism. If there is a principle that would make it possible for me to abandon the world and enter Buddhism, would you explain it to me?"

Dōgen instructed: "This is a difficult problem, not for others to decide. If, after serious consideration, you still have the earnest desire to enter into Buddhism fully and can work out some means to assure the comfort and livelihood of your mother, then it would be a good thing to enter Buddhism, both for your mother and for yourself. Something you want badly enough can always be gained. No matter how fierce the enemy, how remote the beautiful lady, or how carefully guarded the treasure, there is always a means to the goal for the earnest seeker. The unseen help of the guardian gods of heaven and earth assure fulfillment.

"The Sixth Patriarch of Ts'ao-ch'i[9] was a commoner in Hsin-chou and sold firewood to support his mother. One day his mind was stimulated to seek the Way when he heard someone reciting the *Diamond Sutra* in the market place. When he left his mother to go to Huang-p'o,[10] he managed to obtain ten pieces of silver for his mother's food and clothing.

This can be considered a gift from heaven, arising from his earnest desire to enter the Way. Consider this seriously; it is the highest truth.

"If he had waited until his mother's death and then entered Buddhism with no worldly obstacles, it would have conformed to his original intent; and all would have worked out well. But then again, since death is an unpredictable thing, your mother may live a long life, while you may die first. In that case, your plans would have gone awry. You yourself would regret not having entered Buddhism, your mother would be guilty of not having allowed you to do so, and both of you would gather sins rather than benefits. What then?

"If you renounce this life and enter Buddhism, your aged mother might starve to death. But would not the merit of having permitted a son to enter into Buddhism establish a good cause for gaining the Way in the future? If you cast aside the filial love and duty you have not discarded over numerous kalpas and many lives in this life when you have been born in the body of a man and have had the rare opportunity to encounter Buddhism, this would be the mark of one who is truly grateful. How can this not accord with the Buddha's will? It is said that if one son leaves his home to become a monk, seven generations of parents will gain the Way. How can you afford to waste an opportunity for eternal peace because of concern for the body in this present fleeting life? Think this over well for yourselves."

IV

1

*One day following the interviews with his students, Dōgen
instructed:*

Students of the Way, you must not cling to your own
personal views. Even though you may understand, you should
search widely for a good teacher and examine the sayings of
the old Masters if you feel that there is something lacking or
that there is some understanding superior to your own. Yet
you must not cling to the words of the old sages either; they,
too, may not be right. Even if you believe them, you should be
alert so that, in the event that something superior comes
along, you may follow that.

2

On another occasion Dōgen said:

The National Teacher Nan-yang Hui-chung[1] once asked the
attendant priest Lin;[2] "Where do you come from?"

The attendant priest replied: "I come from Ch'eng-nan."

Nan-yang asked: "What is the color of the grass at
Ch'eng-nan?"

"It is yellow," the attendant priest replied.

The teacher then summoned an acolyte and asked him the
same question. The acolyte replied: "It is yellow."

The Master said: "This acolyte, too, deserves to be awarded
a purple robe in front of the bamboo screen and is qualified to
discuss Buddhism with the Emperor. As the teacher of the
Emperor, the acolyte can name the true color of the grass.
Your view does not transcend ordinary common sense."

Shortly thereafter, someone challenged the Master's words,
saying: "The attendant's answer did not transcend common
sense, but what was wrong with that? Just as did the boy, he

named the true color of the grass. He is the one who is the true teacher."

From this we can see the importance of discerning the truth and of not always accepting the words of the ancient Masters. Although it is not good to take a suspicious attitude, it is also a mistake to cling to something that does not deserve faith and not to question a meaning that should be explored.

3

On another occasion Dōgen instructed:

The student must above all separate himself from concepts of the Self. To separate from views of the Self means not to cling to this body. Even though you study deeply the sayings of the old Masters and practice *zazen,* remaining as immobile as stone or iron, you will never gain the Way of the Buddhas and the Patriarchs, even if you try for endless eons, unless you can free yourself from attachment to the body.

No matter how well you say you know the true and provisional teachings or the esoteric and exoteric doctrines, as long as you possess a mind that clings to the body, you will be vainly counting others' treasures, without gaining even half a cent for yourself.

I ask only that you students sit quietly and examine with true insight the beginnings and end of this human body. The body, hair, and skin are the products of the union of our parents. When the breathing stops, the body is scattered amid mountains and fields and finally turns to earth and mud. Why then do you attach to this body?

Viewed from the Buddhist standpoint, the body is no more than the accumulation and dispersal of the eighteen realms of sense.[3] Which realm should we pick out and identify as our body? While differences exist between Zen and other teachings, they agree in that, in the practice of the Way, emphasis is placed on the impermanence of the human body. Once you penetrate this truth, true Buddhism manifests itself clearly.

4

One day Dōgen instructed:

According to an old Master: "If you develop a close relationship with a good man, it is like walking in the fog or dew. Although you do not actually wet your garment, it gradually becomes damp." What he is saying is that if you are close to a good person, you unconsciously become good yourself. This was the case many years ago of the boy who attended Master Chü-chih.[4] There was no way of telling when he studied and practiced, and he himself was unaware of it, but because of the long association with the Master, he gained enlightenment.

If you practice *zazen* as a matter of course for many years, you will suddenly see the vital point of enlightenment and know that *zazen* is the true gate from which to enter.

5

In the second year of Katei, on the evening of the last day of the twelfth month,[5] Dōgen for the first time invited Ejō to take the head seat[6] at Kōshōji. Following an informal sermon, Dōgen had Ejō take up the whisk and lecture to the assembly. This was the first time that the position of meditation director had been filled at Kōshōji.

Dōgen's sermon that day concerned the transmission of Zen:

"The First Patriarch, Bodhidharma,[7] came from the West and stayed at the Shao-lin Temple, awaiting an opportunity to propagate the teaching. He sat gazing patiently at a wall, until Hui-k'o[8] appeared in the last month of the year. Bodhidharma knew that here was a vessel of the Supreme Vehicle,[9] guided him, and later transmitted to him both the robe and the teaching. His descendants spread throughout the world, and the True Law has been handed down to this day.

"For the first time at this monastery, I have today appointed a meditation director and have asked him to take up the whisk and lecture. Don't let the smallness of this assembly or the fact that this is his first lecture bother you. The group around Fen-yang[10] amounted to only six or seven persons; Yao-shan[11] had less than ten disciples under him; yet they all practiced the Way of the Buddhas and the Patriarchs. A time like this, they say, is when a monastery flourishes. Think of those who gained enlightenment upon hearing the sound of bamboo when struck by a tile or on seeing blossoms in bloom.[12] Does the bamboo distinguish the clever or dull, the deluded or enlightened; does the flower differentiate between the shallow and deep, the wise and stupid? Though flowers bloom year after year, not everyone who sees them gains enlightenment. Bamboos always give off sounds, but not all who hear them become enlightened. It is only by the virtue of long study under a teacher and much practice that we gain an affinity with what we have labored for and gain enlightenment and clarity of mind. This does not mean that the sound of bamboo itself has a penetrating effectiveness or that the color of flowers is surpassingly beautiful. Although the sound of bamboo may be wondrous, it does not sound of itself but must wait for the tile that causes the sound to arise; although the color of flowers may be beautiful, they do not bloom of themselves but must wait for the spring wind that opens them.

"In the same way, the study of the Way must have a cause. Although each individual inherently possesses the Way, the gaining of it depends on all the monks studying together. Although an individual may have a brilliant mind, the practice of the Way depends upon the strength of many. Therefore, unifying your minds and concentrating your determination, study under a teacher and seek the Way. Jewels become objects of beauty by polishing; man becomes a true man by training. What jewel is lustrous from the beginning; what person is superior from the outset? You must always keep polishing and always keep training. Do not deprecate yourselves and relax in your study of the Way.

"An old Master has said: 'Do not spend your time wastefully.' I ask you: Is time something that will stop if you value it? Or is it something that cannot be stopped no matter how you value it? This you must understand: it is not time that passes in vain, but people that pass their time in vain. Neither time nor people should be wasted; devote yourselves to the study of the Way.

"In this way, you must all study with the same mind. Although it is not easy to teach Buddhism by myself, if we work together with the same determination, then we will be practicing the Way in the manner of the Buddhas and the Patriarchs. Although most gained enlightenment by following the Tathāgata, there were also those who were enlightened by Ānanda. New meditation director, do not underestimate your ability! Give the assembly a sermon on T'ung-shan's three *kin* of flax."[13]

Dōgen got down from his seat, and as the drum was struck, Ejō took up the whisk and began his sermon. This was Ejō's first sermon at Kōshōji. He was thirty-nine years of age at the time.

6

One day Dōgen instructed:

A layman has remarked: "Is there anyone who does not want fine clothes or who does not hunger for delicious food? Yet those who seek the Way enter distant mountains, sleep amongst the clouds, and endure hunger and cold. Our predecessors certainly suffered, but enduring hardships, they protected the Way. Those who came later heard of their suffering, revered their merits, and longed for the Way."

If even among laymen there are wise men of this sort, then certainly Buddhists must take a similar attitude. Not all the old sages had bones made of metal. Even while Śākyamuni was still alive, his disciples were not all men of superior attainments. If you look at the elaborate regulations of both the Mahāyāna and the Hīnayāna precepts, it is obvious that the monks of the time were moved to perpetrate incredible indiscretions. Yet later they all gained the Way and became Arhats. Although you may be base and inept now, if you arouse the determination to seek the Way and practice, you will succeed. Knowing this, you should immediately give rise to this determination.

The wise men of old all endured hardship and cold, and yet, amidst suffering, they practiced. Students today should force themselves to study the Way, despite the physical hardships and mental anguish they may undergo.

7

Dōgen instructed:

Students cannot gain enlightenment simply because they retain their preconceptions. Without knowing who taught them these things, they consider the mind to be thought and perceptions and do not believe it when they are told that the mind is plants and trees. They think of the Buddha as having marvelous distinguishing marks, with radiance shining from his body, and are shocked when they are told that he is tile and pebble. Such preconceptions were not taught them by their parents, but students come to believe them for no other reason than that they have heard about them from others over a long period of time. Therefore, when the Buddhas and the Patriarchs categorically state that the mind is plants and trees, revise your preconceptions and understand plants and trees as mind. If the Buddha is said to be tile and pebble, consider tile and pebble as the Buddha. If you change your basic preconceptions, you will be able to gain the Way.

An old sage has said: "Although the sun and moon are shining brightly, the floating clouds cover them. Although the clusters of orchids flourish, the autumn wind wilts them."[14] This is quoted in the *Chen-kuan cheng-yao*[15] to indicate a wise king and his evil ministers. I would say that although the floating clouds obscure the sun and moon, it is not for long; although the autumn wind destroys them, the blossoms will open again; although his ministers are evil, if the king is strong in his wisdom, he cannot be overthrown. The same thing applies to Buddhism today. No matter how much evil arises, if we steadfastly protect Buddhism over many long years, the floating clouds will disappear, and the autumn wind will stop.

8

One day Dōgen instructed:

When students are first moved to enter Buddhism, they should read the scriptures and teachings and study them thoroughly, whether they have the mind that seeks the Way or not.

When I was quite young, the realization of the transiency of this world stirred my mind towards seeking the Way.[16] After leaving Mt. Hiei, I visited many temples during my practice of the Way, but until I arrived at Kenninji I had yet to meet a real teacher or a good friend. I was deluded and filled with erroneous thoughts.

The teachers I had seen had advised me first to study until I could be as learned as those who had preceded me. I was told to make myself known to the state and to gain fame in the world. Therefore, even while studying the teachings, what was uppermost in my mind was to become the equal of the ancient wise men of Japan or of those who had gained the title of Great Teacher.[17] But on opening the *Kao-seng chuan* and the *Hsü kao-seng chuan*[18] and on learning about the great priests and Buddhists of China, I could see that their approach differed from those of my teachers. I sensed that the aims with which I had been inspired were looked down upon and despised in all the scriptures and biographical works. By even thinking about fame, I would be disgracing the old men of wisdom and the men of good will to come, while earning a fine name among inferior persons of this period. If I wanted to emulate someone, it should be the former sages and eminent priests of China and India, rather than those of Japan. Feeling shame for the fact that I was not equal to them, I realized that, indeed, I should try to be like the unseen gods of the many heavens and like the Buddhas and the Bodhisattvas. After coming to this understanding, I regarded the great teachers of this country as so much dirt and broken tile. My physical and mental makeup changed completely.

When we look at the actions of the Buddha in his lifetime, we find that he went into the mountains and forests, renouncing his noble rank. Even after his enlightenment, he spent the rest of his life begging for food. The Vinaya says: "Knowing his home was not the true one, he cast it aside and became a monk."

A man of old has said: "Do not in your pride try to emulate the wise men of the past; do not debase yourself and seek to emulate inferior men." The implication here is that both are forms of conceit. Don't forget that even though you may be in a high position now, the time will come when you will fall. Don't forget that, although you may be safe now, danger always lurks. Don't believe that, just because you are alive today, you will still be alive tomorrow. Until you die, imminent death will always be right beneath your feet.

9
On another occasion Dōgen said:
Foolish persons think and say pointless things. At this

temple, there was once an old nun who often talked about her former high position, as though she were ashamed of what she was then doing. Even though people today think of how things used to be, it is of no use whatsoever. This sort of thing seems completely wasteful.

Most people, however, seem to have an inclination towards this type of thinking. It shows the lack of the mind that seeks the Way. By changing this attitude, one may become somewhat like a person who possesses this mind.

Supposing someone has entered the Way but has no trace of the mind that seeks the Way. Because he is a close friend, I want to tell him to pray to the Buddhas and gods to arouse this mind, but I hesitate, thinking that this may make him angry and antagonistic. Yet, unless he arouses this mind, our friendship will be of no use to either of us.

10
Dōgen instructed:

An ancient saying tells us to think about something three times before saying it. This means, of course, that whenever we are about to say or do something, we should think it over three times before expressing it in speech or action. Most Confucians of old understood this to mean to withhold speech or action until a matter had been considered three times and found worthy each time. To the sages of China, considering something three times meant to consider it many times—to think before you speak, to think before you act—and, if what you think is good on each occasion, and only then, to say and do it. Zen monks must take a similar view. What you think or say can lead to unexpected evil. Therefore, you must consider thoroughly whether what you are about to say or do will accord with Buddhism and bring benefits to yourself and others. If you determine it to be good, only then should you speak and act. If the practicer guards this attitude, he will not go against the Buddha mind throughout his lifetime.

When I first entered Kenninji, the monks assembled there dutifully upheld the three conducts.[19] They were careful not to say or do anything that would harm Buddhism or fail to bring benefits to all beings. Even after Eisai's death, while his influence still remained, this practice survived, but now nothing at all is left of it.

Students today must know that they should forget their own bodies and say and do only those things that help Buddhism and bring benefit to themselves and others. If something is of no use, neither say nor do it. When elder monks say or do something, those whose period of service as monks is short should not interrupt. This is a Buddhist regulation and must be considered carefully.

Even laymen have the desire to forget their bodies and seek the Way. Long ago in the land of Chao, there was a person by the name of Lin Hsiang-ju.[20] Though of low birth, he was a man of great talent, and the King of Chao engaged his services to help in the administration of his country.

Once, as an envoy of the King, he was delegated to carry a precious gem, known as the Jewel of Chao, to the land of Ch'in. The King of Ch'in had agreed to exchange fifteen cities for the jewel that Lin Hsiang-ju was charged with carrying. At this time, the other ministers discussed the matter: "To entrust such a valuable jewel to a person of such low birth would make it seem that we have no appropriate person for this duty in our country. It would disgrace us and make us a laughing stock for later generations." They planned to kill Hsiang-ju while he was on his way and to take the jewel from him.

Someone who was aware of the plot secretly advised that Hsiang-ju abandon his mission and save his own life. Hsiang-ju, however, refused: "I won't give up this mission. If later generations hear that I was killed by evil ministers while taking the jewel to Ch'in as an envoy of the King, it would give me joy. While my body might die, my name as a man of wisdom would remain." With these words, he set out on his journey to Ch'in.

When the other ministers heard what he had said, they abandoned their plot. "We cannot kill a man like this," they agreed.

Hsiang-ju finally met the King of Ch'in and presented the jewel to him. He noticed, however, that the King seemed reluctant to exchange his fifteen cities for it. An idea came to

Hsiang-ju, and he said to the King: "There is a flaw in this jewel. Let me show it to you." Taking back the jewel, he continued: "I can tell from your expression that you regret exchanging your fifteen cities for this jewel. Therefore, I shall use my head to break open this jewel against that bronze pillar." Looking at the King with angry eyes, he approached the pillar as if he were really about to break open the jewel.

The King cried out: "Don't break the jewel. I will give the fifteen cities. Keep the jewel until we are able to work out the details." Hsiang-ju then had one of his men return the jewel in secret to his own country.

Later the Kings of Chao and Ch'in met for a party at a place called Min-ch'ih. The King of Chao was an expert on the lute, and the King of Ch'in gave orders that he play it. The King of Chao started at once to play, without first consulting with Hsiang-ju. Enraged that his King had obeyed the orders of the other, he determined to force the King of Ch'in to play the flute. Turning to the King of Ch'in, he said: "You are an expert on the flute and my King has asked to hear you play it." The King of Ch'in refused.

Hsiang-ju then exclaimed: "If you don't play, I'll kill you," and he went towards the King. A Ch'in general grasped his sword and rushed to the defense of his King, but Hsiang-ju glared at him with such malevolence that the general retreated in terror, without drawing his sword. The King of Ch'in agreed to play the flute.

Later Hsiang-ju became a chief minister. In his administration of the country he drew the envy of another minister who did not have equal authority. This other minister sought to kill him, and Hsiang-ju fled, staying in hiding in various parts of the country. He failed to appear at Court when he was due and acted as though he were in abject terror. One of his retainers then said: "It is easy enough to kill that minister. Why do you run away and hide in fear?"

Hsiang-ju replied: "I'm not afraid of him. With my eyes, I forced a Ch'in general to retreat. I took back the jewel from the King of Ch'in. It's not merely a matter of killing a minister. Raising an army and mobilizing troops should be done to defend against enemy attack. The function of the ministers is to protect the country. If we two do not get along and quarrel with each other and if one of us gets killed, then the other is weakened. If this happens, the neighboring country will be delighted to attack us. That is why both of us should keep alive and concern ourselves with protecting the country. Therefore I don't fight with him."

Upon hearing this, the other minister felt great shame. Seeking out Hsiang-ju, he saluted him, and the two became fast friends and cooperated in administering the country.

In this way Hsiang-ju forgot his own body and protected the Way. In protecting Buddhism now, we must have an attitude like his. There is a saying: "It is better to die protecting the Way than to live without it."

11

Dōgen instructed:

It is difficult to determine what is good and what is evil. Laymen say it is good to wear luxurious silks, embroidered garments, and brocades; and bad to wear tattered and discarded rags. But in Buddhism it is the opposite: tattered robes are good and pure; richly embroidered garments are evil and soiled. The same applies to all other things as well.

If someone like me writes a poem that reveals a certain amount of skill in the use of rhyme or words, some laymen may praise me for possessing more than common talents. On the other hand, others may criticize me for having accomplishments unbecoming a monk who has left his home. How can we tell which is good and which is bad?

I have read somewhere: "Things praised and included among pure things are called good; things scorned and included among soiled things are called evil." Elsewhere it is said: "To undergo suffering as recompense for past actions is called bad; to invite comfort as a reward for past actions is called good."

In this way, a detailed consideration must be made: what we find to be really good should be practiced; what we find to be really bad should be discarded. Because monks come from the midst of purity, they consider as good and pure what does not arouse desire among other people.

On another occasion Dōgen said:

Most people in this world say: "I have the desire to study Buddhism; yet the world is degenerate, and man, inferior. The training Buddhism requires is too strenuous for me. I will follow the easy way and merely strengthen my links with Buddhism and put off enlightenment until another life."

The attitude these words express is completely wrong. In Buddhism, the setting-up of the three periods of the Law[21] was merely a temporary expedient.[22] In the Buddha's time, the monks were not necessarily all outstanding; there were some who were extraordinarily depraved and of low character. It was for such evil and inferior persons that the Buddha drew up the precepts. All people inherently have the capacity to awaken to Buddhism. Don't think that they do not possess it. If you practice in accordance with the teachings, you will gain enlightenment without fail.

As long as you have a mind, you can distinguish between good and evil. As long as you have hands and feet, you have the ability to join your palms together and to walk about. Therefore, there is no such thing as not having the equipment to practice Buddhism. All human beings are born with this potential; this is not so of those born in the animal world. Students of the Way, do not wait until tomorrow. This very day, this very moment, practice in accordance with the teaching of the Buddha.

13

Dōgen instructed:

Among laymen there is a saying: "A castle falls when secrets are whispered within its walls." They also say: "A household where two opinions conflict cannot buy even a pin; a household without a conflict of opinion can buy even gold."

Even laymen say that to preserve a household or to defend a castle, there must be unity of purpose if decay is not to set in. How much more so then must monks unite under one teacher, as though milk and water were blended together. We have also the six modes of social harmony.[23] Practicers should not live in their own rooms, keep aloof from each other, and study Buddhism themselves as they see fit. It is like crossing the ocean aboard a single ship. With the same mind, they must conduct themselves with a mutual dignity, correcting mistakes and selecting the good, and practicing Buddhism in the same way. This has been the method that has come down to us from the Buddha's time.

14
Dōgen instructed:
When Zen Master Fang-hui of Mt. Yang-ch'i[24] first became the chief priest, the monastery was old and dilapidated, which caused the monks many difficulties. At that time, the monk in charge of temple affairs suggested that the buildings be repaired.

Fang-hui said: "The buildings may be dilapidated, but it is better than living on the bare ground or under a tree. If one part needs repair and if the roof leaks, then do *zazen* somewhere where the rain does not come in. If monks can gain enlightenment by the construction of temple buildings, then we should make them of gold and jewels. Enlightenment does not depend on the quality of the place you stay in but only on the degree to which your *zazen* is effective."

The next day Fang-hui preached to the assembly in the lecture hall:

"On becoming the chief priest at Mt. Yang-ch'i, I find the roof and walls crumbling. On all the floors, pearls of snow are blowing. The monks pull in their necks from the cold and sigh." After a pause he continued: "It reminds me of the old sages who sat under the trees."

This attitude is not found in Buddhism alone; we find it in the art of governing as well. Emperor T'ai-tsung of the T'ang refused to build a new palace, preferring to live in the old one instead.

The Zen Master Lung-ya[25] said: "To study Buddhism, you must first study poverty. Only after learning poverty and becoming really poor can you become intimate with the Way." From the ancient days of the Buddha until now, I have neither seen nor heard of any student of the Way who possessed wealth.

One day a visiting priest said: "Recently, the method of renouncing the world seems to be to prepare a supply of food and other necessities in advance so that one does not have to worry afterwards. This is a small thing, but it helps in the study of the Way. If such items are lacking, practice is disrupted. But, according to what you have said, there should be no such preparation, and everything should be left to fate. If this is really so, won't trouble arise later? What do you think?"

Dōgen answered: "For this we have the precedents of all the former Masters. This is not just my personal view; the Buddhas and the Patriarchs in India and China all followed a similar method. At no time is the blessing of the curl on the Buddha's forehead[26] used up. Why should I plan my life? It is not easy to determine and plan for tomorrow. What I do now has all been done before by the Buddhas and the Patriarchs; it is not something that I do because of personal concepts. If food becomes scarce and there is nothing to eat, only then look for a means to solve the situation. There is no need to think about it in advance.

16

Dōgen instructed:

I have heard it told but don't know whether it is true or not that, when the late Chūnagon, Jimyōin,[27] became a priest, a valuable sword of his was stolen. A warrior in his service investigated, found the sword, and informed Chūnagon that the thief was another warrior in his retinue. Chūnagon, however, denied that the sword was his and had it returned.

Without a doubt, it was the stolen sword, but, thinking about the disgrace to the warrior who had stolen it, Chūnagon denied that it was his. Although everybody knew the truth of the situation, the matter ended without incident. Because of this, the descendants of Chūnagon flourished. If even a layman has this attitude, how much more so then should monks possess it!

Because monks have no personal property, they make wisdom and virtue their treasures. If someone who is without the mind that seeks the Way does something bad, do not let your expression show your displeasure; nor condemn him for doing evil. Just explain things to him in such a way that he does not become angry. It is said that something that encourages violence does not last long. Although you may be correct in your censure of someone, your very correctness does not last long if you use harsh words. A petty person takes offense at the slightest criticism, thinking that he has been insulted. This is not true of a superior person, for even when he is struck, he does not think of retaliation. Today in our country, there are numerous petty people. You must be careful.

V

1

One day Dōgen instructed:

Do not be reluctant to give up your life for the sake of
Buddhism. With the Way in mind, even laymen have cast away
their lives, disregarded their families, and dedicated
themselves to loyalty. Such people are known as loyal
ministers and men of wisdom.

Long ago, when Kao-tsung[1] of the Han Dynasty went to war
with a neighboring country, the mother of one of his ministers
was in enemy territory. The military leaders suspected this
minister of having double loyalties, and Kao-tsung himself
also wondered whether this man, thinking of his mother, might
not go over to the enemy. Should such a thing happen, there
was the chance that the war might be lost. At the same time,
the mother, fearing that her son might return for her sake,
cautioned him: "Don't relax your loyalties because of me. If I
continue to live, you may have a divided mind," and she threw
herself upon a sword and died. It is said that her son, who
from the outset had no divided loyalties, deepened his
determination to dedicate himself to his duties in battle.

The Zen monk is truly in accord with Buddhism when he is
completely without a divided mind. In Buddhism there are
some who are endowed with compassion and wisdom from
the outset. Yet even though these qualities may not be present
from the beginning, they can be acquired by study. Don't
cling arbitrarily to your own views. Just cast aside both body
and mind, plunge into the great sea of Buddhism, and entrust
yourself to the Buddhist teachings.

During the reign of Kao-tsung of the Han Dynasty, a wise
minister said: "Remedying the disturbances of government is

like unraveling a knotted rope. Don't hurry, but first examine the knot carefully and then undo it."

It is the same with Buddhism. Practice carefully and come to understand the principles of Buddhism. Those who best understand the Buddhist teachings are always those with the mind that seeks the Way intensely. No matter how clever or brilliant, those without this mind can neither free themselves from egoistic desires nor forsake fame and profit. They cannot become true Buddhists; nor can they understand the True Law.

2
Dōgen instructed:

Students of the Way must not study Buddhism for the sake of themselves. They must study Buddhism only for the sake of Buddhism. The key to this is to renounce both body and mind without holding anything back and to offer them to the great sea of Buddhism. Next you must vigorously undertake even what is difficult to do and difficult to endure, without concerning yourself at all with right and wrong and without clinging to your own opinions. You must cast aside anything that does not accord with the Buddhist truth, even though it be something you most earnestly desire. Never attempt, through the virtue of your practice of Buddhism, to gain something good in recompense. Once you have committed yourself to Buddhism, there is no need to reflect again on yourself. Just practice in accordance with the rules of Buddhism and refrain from getting caught up in personal views. This has all been proven in the past. If your mind does not seek anything, then you will gain a great peace.

Among the laity, there are those who never have associated with others and have grown up only in their own homes. They behave arbitrarily as they please and give precedence to their own opinions, not caring what others may see and think. Such persons are always bad. In studying the Way, be careful of things like these. You will become a true Buddhist easily if you work closely with others, follow your teacher, do not set up your own views, and make new your own mind.

In studying the Way, the first thing you must do is to understand poverty. If you cast aside fame and profit, curry favor with no one, and discard all things, you will certainly become a good monk. In China those who were known as good monks were all poor. Their robes were torn, and everything about them was impoverished.

When I was at Mt. T'ien-t'ung, the recorder at the temple was named Tao-ju. He was the son of the Prime Minister, but, because he had separated from his family and did not covet worldly profit, his robes were tattered, and people could scarcely bear to look at him. But he was renowned for his virtue and had become the recorder of a great temple.

Once I asked him: "You are the son of an official and a member of a wealthy family. Why are the things you wear so coarse and miserable?"

"Because I became a monk," he replied.

3

One day Dōgen instructed:

A layman has said: "Treasures often become an enemy that bring harm to the body. This was so in the past, and it is so now."

The story that occasioned this remark was as follows: Once there was a commoner who had a beautiful wife. A local lord demanded the woman, but her husband refused to surrender her. The lord then called up his troops and surrounded their home. When the wife was about to be taken away, the husband said: "Because of you, I am losing my life." The wife replied: "Because of you, I shall cast aside my life," and she leaped from the tall building and died. Later the husband managed to escape, and he was able to tell the story.

Once there was a wise man who administered a province as a government official. His son was obliged to leave on state business, and he went to bid his father farewell. As he was going, his father presented him with a bolt of silk.

The son said: "You are a man of high integrity. Where did you get this silk?"

The father replied: "I bought it from what was left over from my salary."

The son proceeded to the capital, where he told this story to the Emperor. The Emperor was greatly impressed by the father's wisdom. The son said: "My father has up to now managed to keep his name hidden. Now I have made it known. My father's wisdom is indeed superior to mine."

The point of this story is that, while a bolt of silk is a trivial thing, the wise man knows that he should not make private use of public property. But the really wise man concealed his talents and merely remarked that the gift was quite correct, because it came out of his own salary. When we have laymen like this, how much more so then should the Zen monk possess a mind that seeks nothing for itself. People who truly follow the Way would do well to conceal the fact that they are Buddhists.

Dōgen again said:

Someone once asked a Taoist sage: "How does one become a sage?"

He answered: "If you want to become a sage, just like the Way of the sages."

Therefore, if students want to attain the Way of the Buddhas and the Patriarchs, they must like the Way of the Buddhas and the Patriarchs.

4

Dōgen instructed:

In ancient times there was a king who, after bringing a stable government to his country, inquired of his ministers: "I have governed the country well. Does this make me a wise king?"

The ministers replied: "You have governed the country well. You are very wise indeed."

One minister, however, replied: "You are not wise." When the king asked why, the minister answered: "When you came into power, you gave land to your sons but none to your younger brother." The king was displeased and had the minister banished.

Later the king asked another minister: "Am I benevolent?" When told that he was, the king asked why this was so.

The minister said: "A benevolent ruler always has loyal ministers, and loyal ministers give outspoken advice. The minister you banished gave this kind of advice, and he was a loyal minister. If the king were not benevolent, he would not have had a person like that." The king was deeply impressed and recalled the former minister.

Dōgen again said:
During the time of the First Emperor of the Ch'in,[2] a prince made plans to enlarge his gardens. A minister commented: "A splendid idea. If you enlarge the gardens, all sorts of birds and beasts will gather there, and then we can defend ourselves against the neighboring armies with troops of birds and beasts." With these words, the garden project was dropped.

On another occasion, the prince proposed building a palace with lacquered pillars. The minister remarked: "This is fine. By lacquering the pillars, you can stop the enemy from entering." Again the project was dropped.

The essence of Confucianism is to check the bad and encourage the good by the skillful use of words. Zen monks, when guiding others, must also adopt skillfulness such as this.

5

One day a priest asked: "Which is better, a wise person without the mind that seeks the Way or a person with no wisdom who possesses such a mind?"

Dōgen answered: "In many cases, the person who is without wisdom but who possesses the mind that seeks the Way will eventually retrogress, whereas he who is wise but without it will eventually awaken to this mind. There are many examples of this in the world today. Therefore, do not concern yourself with whether you possess this mind, but just concentrate on the study of the Way.

"In order to study the Way, you must be poor. In both Buddhist and secular works, we find examples: some persons were so poor that they had no home to live in; others like Ch'ü Yüan, drowned in the Ts'ang-lang River;[3] some hid in Mt. Shou-yang;[4] some practiced *zazen* under trees and on the bare ground; and others built crude shelters among tombs or in mountain wildernesses. Again, there were people who were wealthy, with many possessions, who built palaces adorned with red lacquer, gold, and precious stones. Stories of such people are also written in books. But in these examples, the people who are praised and set up as models to encourage later men were all poor with no possessions. When it comes to cautioning against evil conduct, those who possessed wealth and luxurious properties are censured for having been men of extravagance."

6

Dōgen instructed:

Monks must never delight in receiving public donations; yet they must not decline them either. The late Abbot Eisai said: "To enjoy receiving public donations does not accord with Buddhist regulations. To take no joy does not accord with the heart of the donor." The traditional view is that offerings are made not to the monk himself but to the Three Treasures. Therefore, you must say to the donor: "The Three Treasures will surely accept your offering."

7

Dōgen instructed:

In ancient times it was said: "A gentleman is stronger than an ox, but he does not struggle with an ox." Students today, even though they feel that their wisdom and talents are superior, should not delight in arguing with others. Do not abuse others with harsh words or glare at them with angry eyes. Although people today give substantial donations and render favors, they are apt to react against you if they detect an expression of anger on another's face or if they are criticized with harsh words.

Once the priest Chen-ching K'o-wen[5] told his assembly: "Some time ago, when Hsüeh-feng[6] and I were studying together, we made a pact of friendship with each other. One day Hsüeh-feng was arguing about the teachings with another student in the monks' dormitory. They argued in loud voices and finally began fighting, using exceedingly abusive language towards each other. When the argument was over, Hsüeh-feng took me to task: 'We are fellow students of like mind. We have even made a firm pact with each other. Why didn't you help me out when I was fighting with that fellow?' All I could do at the time was to bow my head in regret.

"Later Hsüeh-feng became an excellent teacher, and I

became the priest of this temple. When I think back on the incident now, Hsüeh-feng's argument served no useful purpose whatsoever. Indeed, it is always a mistake to argue. Because I believed argument to be pointless, I had remained silent."

Students should consider this thoroughly now. If you have the determination to study the Way, you must do so, begrudging any time wasted. When do you have the time to argue with people? It won't do you or anyone else any good in the long run. If this is so with Buddhist teachings, how much more useless it is to argue about ordinary worldly affairs!

"A gentleman is stronger than an ox, but he does not struggle with an ox." Even if you think that you know the teaching thoroughly and are far superior to your adversary, you should not overwhelm him with argument.

But if a sincere seeker after Buddhism asks you about the teaching, do not begrudge him an answer. Explain it to him for his sake. But for three questions, give only one answer; long-winded dissertations are worthless. After reading Chen-ching's words, I realized that I myself was at fault here. Taking his words to heart, I stopped arguing about the teaching with others.

8
Dōgen instructed:

The old Masters frequently warn: "Do not spend time wastefully" and "do not pass your time in vain." Students today should begrudge every moment of time. This dewlike life fades away; time speeds swiftly. In this short life of ours, avoid involvement in superfluous things and just study the Way.

People nowadays say: "It is difficult to discard the obligations to our parents," or "It is difficult to disobey the orders of a master," or "It is difficult to part from wives, children, and relatives." Or else they say: "It is difficult to guarantee the livelihood of my relatives," or "People will revile me if I forsake my home." Or again they say: "I am too poor to buy the equipment for the monastic life," or "I don't have the capacity to endure the study of the Way." Thinking in this way, they join the worldly pursuit of wealth and property, without separating from master or parents and without severing from their wives, children, and relatives. With their whole life wasted, they will have only regrets when they face the end.

Sit calmly and consider the principles of Buddhism; and quickly determine to arouse the mind that seeks the Way. Masters and parents cannot give you enlightenment. Wives, children, and relatives cannot save you from suffering. Wealth and property cannot free you from the cycle of birth and death. Ordinary people cannot help you. If you do not practice now, claiming you are without the capacity, when will you ever be able to attain the Way? Single-mindedly, study the Way without giving thought to the myriad things. Don't put it off until later.

9

Dōgen instructed:

In studying the Way, separate from considerations of the Self. Even though you study all the *sūtra*s and *śāstra*s, if you cannot cut off attachments to the self, you will inevitably fall into the realm of evil demons. A man of old has said: "If you don't have the body and mind of the Buddhadharma, how can you become a Buddha or a Patriarch?"

To separate from the Self means to throw your body and mind into the great sea of Buddhism and to practice in accordance with Buddhism, no matter what the hardship or anxiety may be. You may feel that begging for food demeans you in the eyes of others, but you will never be able to enter into Buddhism as long as you think in this way. Forget all worldly views and study the Way, relying only on the Truth. To think that you are unsuitable for Buddhism because of your inferior capacity reveals an attachment to the Self. To concern yourself with the opinions and reactions of others is the basis of self-attachment. Just study Buddhism. Don't follow the sentiments of the world.

10

One day Ejō asked: "How should those in a Zen monastery conduct themselves in the study of Buddhism?"

Dōgen instructed: "Just practice *zazen.* Wherever you are,

whether in an upper floor or downstairs, just practice Zen meditation. Instead of gossiping idly with others, always sit alone like a person deaf and dumb."

11

One day, following a sermon, Dōgen instructed:

Ta-tao Ku-ch'üan[7] said: "I sit facing the wind; I sleep facing the sun. I am far more comfortable than the people today who wear richly embroidered robes." These are the words of an old Master, yet they are open to some doubt. By "people today" does he mean those who covet worldly profit? If so, they are scarcely worthy of comparison. Why even mention them? Or does he mean people who are studying Buddhism? If so, why say they are more comfortable than those who are wearing richly embroidered robes? If you look at the attitude behind this statement, it would seem that he valued richly embroidered robes. A sage is not like this. He clings neither to gold and jewels nor to tile and pebble. That is why Śākyamuni ate the milk-gruel offered by a milk-maid as well as grain meant for horses. They were both the same to him.

In Buddhism there is no light and heavy; it is man who discriminates the shallow and deep. In this world there are some who would refuse to accept a jewel if it were offered as a valuable object, whereas they would gladly accept and treasure something of wood and stone if they were told it was of no value. The jewel originally came from the earth; wood and stone are produced by the great earth. Why is one not accepted because it is valuable, and the other accepted and treasured because it is cheap? Can it be because the desire to accept the valuable thing would indicate attachment? Yet if the cheap object is accepted and cherished, the fault is still the same. This is something that students must be careful about.

12

Dōgen instructed:

When the late Master Myōzen[8] was about to go to China, his teacher Myōyū[9] of Mt. Hiei became seriously ill and lay on his death bed.

At this time Myōyū said: "I'm suffering the diseases of old

age and am about to die. Please put off going to China now, care for me in my final sickness, conduct services for me, and carry out your original plan after I have gone."

Myōzen then called together his disciples and fellow priests and consulted with them. "After leaving my parents' home in childhood," he said, "I grew up under the care of this teacher and am deeply obligated to him. From him I learned the doctrines of Buddhism, the literature of the Mahāyāna and Hīnayāna, and the provisional and real teachings. He fostered my understanding of causality and right and wrong and enabled me to exceed my colleagues and to gain fame. Even my discernment of the principles of Buddhism and the arousing of my determination to cross over to China in search of the True Law stem from his kindness. But this year he has suddenly aged and now lies ill on his death bed. He has only a short time left to live and, I shall never see him again if I leave now. For these reasons he has strongly urged me to put off my trip. It is difficult to disobey a teacher's request. But my going to China now at the risk of my life to seek the Way also derives from the great compassion of the Bodhisattva and the desire to benefit all beings. Is there any justification for disobeying my teacher's wishes and going to China? Tell me how all of you feel about it."

All his disciples replied: "Give up going to China this year. Your teacher is very close to death; he cannot last long. If you just stay this year and go to China the next, you will not have opposed your teacher's wishes or neglected your obligations. What prevents you from putting off your trip for six months or a year? If you do, you will not be breaking the close ties between master and disciple and will still be able to go through with your original plans to visit China."

Although at this time I was the least experienced of the monks, I said: "If you feel that your Buddhist enlightenment is adequate now, it would be better to put off your trip."

Myōzen said: "That is so. If Buddhist practice reaches this stage, it should be good enough. If I practice like this for the rest of my life, I think it would be possible to break free from delusion and gain the Buddhist Way."

"If that is so, then stop your trip," I said.

After each had expressed his opinion and the discussion

was over, Myōzen said: "You all seem to agree that I should stay, but my view differs. Even if I were to stay now, it would not prolong the life of a dying man. Even if I were to stay and take care of him, I could not stop his suffering. Even if I were to comfort him in his final hours, it would not have anything to do with his escape from the cycle of birth and death. All this would amount to would be to comfort my teacher in accordance with his request. It would be of absolutely no use in separating from the world and gaining the Way. If my determination to seek the Law is mistakenly obstructed, it will become the source of evil acts. But, if I can carry out my determination to visit China in search of the Law and can gain even a trace of enlightenment, it will serve to awaken many people, even though it means opposing the deluded wishes of one person. If the virtue gained were exceptional, it would serve to repay the kindness of my teacher. Even if I should die while crossing the sea and fail in my original plan, since my death would stem from my determination to seek the Law, my vow would not be exhausted in any future life. Think of the results of Hsüan-tsang's[10] journey to India. To waste precious time just for the sake of one person does not accord with the Buddha's will. I have, therefore, definitely decided to go to China now." With these words Myōzen set out for China.

From his words I could tell that Myōzen truly possessed the mind that seeks the Way. Students today must not do useless things and spend their time in vain, whether for the sake of parents or of teachers. They should not put aside Buddhism, the most excellent of all teachings, and waste their days away.

At that time Ejō asked: "In truly seeking the Law, it is undoubtedly necessary to renounce completely the ties of worldly obligation that bind us to parents and teachers in this world of delusion. Even if we completely cast aside obligations and affections towards parents and teachers when we consider the activities of a Bodhisattva, should we not set aside benefits for ourselves and work for the benefit of others? Since there was no one else to nurse his teacher in the infirmities of his old age, wasn't it contrary to the Bodhisattva conduct for Myōzen to think only of his own practice and not take care of his teacher when he was in a position to help him? A Bodhisattva must not discriminate in his good deeds.

Do we base our understanding of Buddhism on what the circumstances or the occasion may be? Under this principle, should he not have stayed and helped him? Why should he not help his old and infirm teacher, instead of thinking only of his own desire to seek the Law? What is your opinion?"

Dōgen instructed: "In both benefiting others and practicing yourself, to discard the inferior and retain the superior comprise the good action of the Bodhisattva. To offer a diet of beans and water in an effort to save the old and infirm merely caters to the misguided love and deluded passions of this brief life. If you turn your back on the deluded emotions and study the Way that leads to enlightenment, even though you may have cause for some regret, you will establish an excellent basis for transcending the world. Consider this well, consider this well!"

13

One day Dōgen instructed:

Many people in this world say: "I hear the words of the teacher, but they do not agree with what I think." This view is mistaken. I do not know what is in their minds. Can they be thinking that the principles of the sacred teachings are wrong because they do not agree with what they themselves imagine? This is sheer idiocy. Or are the words spoken by the teacher unsuited to their own minds? If so, why do they ask the teacher in the first place? Or do they say this on the basis of their own ordinary emotional concepts? If so, this emotional concept is nothing but the deluded mind that has come down from the beginningless beginning to the present.

The key to studying the Way is to discard all conceptions of the Self you have held up to now and to regenerate yourself completely by following the sacred writings, even if they do not happen to agree with your beliefs. This has always been the one essential to the study of the Way.

A few years ago when I was studying, among my fellow students was one who clung firmly to his own beliefs. He visited many Zen masters, but he wasted his life and failed to understand Buddhism because he rejected what did not suit his mind and accepted only what agreed with his own preconceptions. This made me realize that the study of the

Way must never be approached with this attitude. With this in mind, I followed the words of the teacher and awakened fully to the truth. Later I found the following passage in one of the *sūtras* I read: "If you want to study Buddhism, do not bring with you the conditioned mind of the past, present, and future." I knew for certain that I must forget the various views and opinions accumulated from the past and that I must gradually reform myself.

A secular work says: "Loyal words are harsh to the ears."[11] This means that valuable advice often offends one's ears. Even if disagreeable, such advice, if firmly followed, will ultimately be of value.

14

One day, following a talk on various subjects, Dōgen said:

From the outset, there is neither good nor evil in the human mind. Good and evil arise according to circumstances. For example, when a man wishes to study Buddhism and retreats to the woods, he finds the quiet of the forest good and the busy world of man evil. Then when he becomes bored and his resolve weakened, he leaves the forest, for he now finds that it is bad. In other words, the mind has no fixed characteristic; good and evil depend on the circumstance. Thus, if you meet good circumstances, your mind will become good and, if you are involved in bad circumstances, your mind will become bad. Don't think that the mind is inherently bad. Just follow the circumstances.

15

On another occasion Dōgen instructed:

I believe that the human mind is constantly influenced by the words of others. In the *Mahāprajñāpāramitā śāstra*[12] we read: "Supposing a foolish man holds a precious jewel in his hand and hears someone remark: 'How vulgar you are to hold things in your own hands.' He thinks: 'This jewel is precious, but my reputation is also important. I don't want to be thought an inferior person.' Worrying about this, he concerns himself with his reputation to such an extent that the words of others make him throw away his jewel, as though he wanted someone else to pick it up. In the end he loses his jewel."

So it is with the mind of man. A person may think that something is undoubtedly good for him, yet he gives it up because he is worried about his own reputation. Then again, while aware that something is completely bad for him, a person will pursue it nonetheless for the sake of fame and profit. When following good and evil, the mind is pulled along by the good and evil. Therefore, no matter how bad your mind may have been in the past, if you follow a good Zen teacher, you come to resemble a good man, and your mind naturally becomes good. If you associate with a bad person, even though you know from the beginning in your own mind that it is bad, you eventually become evil yourself, as you fall unwittingly under his influence.

Again, the human mind, even though determined not to let others take something, will reluctantly offer it if asked strongly enough. On the other hand, a person may be determined to give something but in the end will not do so because of the lack of opportunity or occasion.

Therefore, the student, even though he may not possess the mind that seeks the Way, should associate with a good person, become involved in good circumstances, and hear and see the same thing any number of times. Don't think that, because you have heard or seen something once, there is no need to hear or see it again. For those who have already aroused the mind that seeks the Way, each hearing serves to polish the mind and make for progress, even though the subject may be the same. Those who do not have this mind may not gain very much on the first or second hearing, but if they keep listening steadily, it will slowly soak in, as a garment that gradually gets damp from walking through the fog and dew. If they hear the words of a good person many times, shame naturally arises for not having the mind that seeks the Way, and that mind will truly arise of itself. Therefore, no matter how familiar they are to you, you must look at the sacred scriptures many times. Although you may have heard the words of your teacher many times, you must listen to them again and again. Gradually your mind will be stirred to greater depths. Do not repeatedly draw near to anything that hinders the practice of the Way. No matter how painful or difficult it may be, draw near to a good friend and practice the Way.

16

Dōgen instructed:

The Zen Master Ta-hui[13] once had a growth on his buttocks. A doctor examined him and found it extremely dangerous. Ta-hui asked: "If it's this serious, am I going to die?"

"There's a good chance that you will," the doctor answered.

"If I'm going to die, I had better practice *zazen* with even greater effort," Ta-hui said. He concentrated on *zazen,* the growth broke open, and that was all there was to the matter.

The minds of the men of old were like this. When they became sick, they practiced *zazen* all the more vigorously. People nowadays who are perfectly well must not take a relaxed attitude to the practice of *zazen.* I suspect that the occurrence of illness stems from the mind. If you lie to a hiccuping person and put him on the defensive, he gets so involved in explaining himself that his hiccups stop. Some years ago when I went to China, I suffered from diarrhea while aboard ship. A violent storm arose, causing great confusion; before I knew it, my sickness was gone. This makes me think that if we concentrate on study and forget about other things, illness will not arise.

17

Dōgen instructed:

There is a popular proverb: "Unless he behaves as though deaf and dumb, a man cannot become the head of a house." This means that a person who does not heed to the slanders of others and who says nothing critical about their shortcomings will be able to accomplish his own work. Such a man deserves to become the head of a house. This may be only a popular proverb, but it applies to the conduct of Zen monks as well. How does one practice the Way without reacting to the scorn or hatred of others and without saying anything good or bad about them? Only those who have penetrated to the very bone and marrow are able to accomplish this.

18

Dōgen instructed:

The Zen Master Ta-hui has stated: "In studying Buddhism you must have the attitude of a man who has borrowed a vast sum of money and then is asked to repay it at a time when he has nothing. If you are able to have a mind such as this, it is easy to gain the Way."

Dōgen continued:

The *Hsin-hsin ming*[14] says: "To achieve the Way is not difficult; just reject discrimination." If you cast aside the mind that discriminates, then at once you gain awakening. To abandon the discriminating mind means to break free from the Self. Do not think that studying Buddhism for the profit you may gain is a substitute for the practice of Buddhism. Just practice Buddhism for the sake of Buddhism. Even though you study a thousand *sūtras* and ten thousand *śāstras* and sit so hard that you break through the *zazen* seat, you cannot gain the Way of the Buddhas and the Patriarchs without this determination. Just cast aside body and mind, and, if within Buddhism you have no biased preconceptions, you will attain awakening at once.

19

Dōgen instructed:

An old Master has stated: "In a Zen monastery, all properties and grain supplies are placed in charge of superintendents, who understand cause and effect and who delegate the actual work to the appropriate persons. This means that the Zen Master of the monastery does not concern himself with major or minor administrative problems but encourages the assembly in intensive *zazen* and *kōan* meditation.

Again it is said: "To embody a little art is better than owning huge tracts of rich land." "In giving, do not expect anything in return, and do not regret what you have given to others." "If you can keep your mouth as silent as your nose, you will invite no trouble." "If a man's actions are noble, others will naturally respect him, but if a man's learning is great, others will soon overtake him." "If you plow deep and plant shallow, you invite disaster from heaven. If you benefit yourself and harm others, how can you avoid evil retribution?"

When students of the Way examine the kōan, they must

study them closely, concentrating full attention and utmost effort.

20

Dōgen instructed:

An old Master has said: "Take one step beyond the top of a hundred-foot pole." This means that you must cast away both body and mind, as though climbing to the top of a hundred-foot pole and letting go of with both hands and feet. There are several important points in this regard.

Nowadays some people seem to have renounced the world and left their homes, but, when one examines their conduct, they have truly neither renounced the world nor left their homes. The first requisite for one who leaves his home to become a monk is to separate from the Self and from all desires for fame and profit. Anyone who cannot accomplish this separation may practice with the intensity of someone brushing fire from his burning head and display zealousness comparable to the Buddha's raising his foot,[15] yet all this will amount to is merely senseless hardship, and he will never escape the world. Even in China there were men who renounced hard-to-renounce family ties and abandoned hard-to-abandon worldly goods to enter a Zen monastery. Some even occupied the position of chief temple priest, and yet, because they practiced without knowing this ancient truth, they wasted their lives without awakening to the Way or making clear their own minds. This occurs because some people, even though they have at the outset aroused the mind that seeks the Way and become monks and disciples of good teachers, do not think of becoming Buddhas and Patriarchs but concern themselves with letting the patrons and donors know of the high standing of themselves and their temples. They speak of this to their relatives and seek to gain reverence and offerings from others. In addition, they demean the integrity of other monks, in an attempt to give the impression that they alone have the mind that seeks the Way and that only they are good. Such men are not worth talking about any further and are comparable to the five evil unbelieving monks.[16] There is no doubt that they will fall into hell. Laymen,

---

unaware of the situation, sometimes consider them to be fine individuals with minds that seek the Way.

There are others who are somewhat better than these people. Without coveting the offerings of donors, they enter a Zen monastery and practice, cutting their ties with parents, wives, and children. Yet by nature, they are lazy, although they are ashamed of appearing indolent. Thus, they pretend to be practicing when the chief priest and the monks in charge of meditation are watching. When unobserved, however, they take every opportunity to idle away their time. They are perhaps better than laymen who conduct themselves in an improper manner, but they are still unable to cast aside the Self and desire for fame and profit.

Then again there are others who are not constrained by what the Master might think and do not worry whether they are seen or not by the supervising priests or their fellow students. Thinking, "Buddhism is not for others but for myself alone," they earnestly strive to become Buddhas and Patriarchs in their own bodies. They can be considered as far more versed in Buddhism than those described above, but, because they practice thinking only of becoming good themselves, they have yet to break free from the Self. They yearn to gain the approval of the various Buddhas and Bodhisattvas and to perfect their own enlightenment. They, too, are unable to cast aside the mind that seeks personal satisfaction and pursues fame and profit.

All these various types of persons, even if they have climbed to the top of a hundred-foot pole, cannot let go; they still cling to it. Those who just throw their bodies and minds into Buddhism and practice without even thinking of gaining enlightenment can be called unstained practicers. This is what is meant by "not stopping where the Buddha is and walking quickly past where the Buddha is not."[17]

21

Dōgen instructed:

Do not make arrangements in advance for obtaining your clothing and food. If all the food is gone, then you may go out and beg for some. To make plans in advance to beg for food from certain persons is like storing up provisions, which violates the Buddhist regulations. Monks are like the clouds and have no fixed abode. Like flowing water, they attach themselves to nothing. Even though monks possess nothing but their robes and bowl, if they rely on even one donor or on one household of relatives, they and those upon whom they rely become enmeshed, and the food is thus unclean. With the body and mind nourished by such tainted food, an awakening to the Great Law of the various Buddhas cannot be expected. For example, just as things stained by the indigo plant become blue and those stained by the *kihada* become yellow, so a body and mind stained by food procured by illegitimate means become a contaminated body. To seek Buddhism with such a body and mind is like pressing sand to get oil. On each occasion, always think in terms of how things will conform with the principles of Buddhism. Plans made in advance all violate against the Buddha Way. Consider this well.

22
Dōgen instructed:

All students should know that each person has a shortcoming. Of the shortcomings people have, the greatest is arrogance. Buddhist and secular works both caution against it.

A non-Buddhist work says: "There are some who are poor yet do not curry favor, but there is none who is rich who is not arrogant." This warns against the tendency of the wealthy towards self-pride. It makes an important point, one worth considering well.

For those of low status, it is the height of arrogance to think of equaling the upper classes or of excelling them. This sort of thing, however, is relatively easy to caution against. Someone in the lay world who has abundant wealth and property and enjoys good fortune is acknowledged by his relatives and associates. But because of the pride that accompanies this, the lower classes who witness it become resentful. How can a wealthy person be discreet in terms of inflicting this sort of pain on others? It is difficult to caution a wealthy person, and he will scarcely practice self-restraint himself. Again, this person may have no intention of showing arrogance; yet, as he goes innocently about his own business, he arouses envy and hurt among the less fortunate people around him. To impose self-restraint here is to be discreet in regard to one's pride. Those who consider their wealth as a just reward and who pay no attention to the envy of the poor are called arrogant.

In a non-Buddhist text it is written: "Do not pass before the home of a poor man while riding in a carriage." The implication is that, even though a person can afford to ride in a fine carriage, he should use discretion in front of the poor. Buddhist scriptures also make this point.

Students and monks these days think that they excell others because of their knowledge of the teachings. Never take pride in such a thing. It is the height of arrogance to call attention to the errors of those beneath you or to criticize your seniors and colleagues for their mistakes.

An old Master has said: "It is all right to be defeated in front of the wise but never win in front of the foolish."

Even though someone misunderstands what you know to be true, you yourself err if you point out his mistake. In discussing the Buddhist teachings, do not ridicule your predecessors and seniors. Be especially careful of this on occasions when you may arouse the envy and jealousy of the unlearned and ignorant.

When I stayed at Kenninji, many people asked about the Buddhist doctrines. Their questions revealed their own shortcomings and mistakes, but, fully aware of the need for caution, I talked only about the merits of the teachings themselves. Since I did not make a point of picking out the mistakes of others, nothing untoward happened. The foolish, with their deep-rooted preconceptions, would surely become angry, saying: "You are criticizing my teacher for his shortcomings." The wise person with a true understanding, because he comprehends the meaning of Buddhism, discerns his own mistakes and those of his teachers without being told, and he takes the necessary corrective steps. These things must be thoroughly understood.

23
Dōgen instructed:

The most important point in the study of the Way is *zazen*. Many people in China gained enlightenment solely through the strength of *zazen*. Some who were so ignorant that they could not answer a single question exceeded the learned who had studied many years solely through the efficacy of their single-minded devotion to *zazen*. Therefore, students must concentrate on *zazen* alone and not bother about other things. The Way of the Buddhas and Patriarchs is *zazen* alone. Follow nothing else.

At that time Ejō asked: "When we combine *zazen* with the reading of the texts, we can understand about one point in a hundred or a thousand upon examining the Zen sayings and the *kōan*. But in *zazen* alone there is no indication of even this much. Must we devote ourselves to *zazen* even then?"

Dōgen answered: "Although a slight understanding seems to emerge from examining the *kōan*, it causes the Way of the Buddhas and the Patriarchs to become even more distant. If you devote your time to doing *zazen* without wanting to know anything and without seeking enlightenment, this is itself the Patriarchal Way. Although the old Masters urged both the reading of the scriptures and the practice of *zazen*, they clearly emphasized *zazen*. Some gained enlightenment through the *kōan*, but the merit that brought enlightenment came from the *zazen*. Truly the merit is in the *zazen*.

VI

1

Dōgen instructed:

If you must be bothered by criticism, be bothered by the criticism of an enlightened man.

When I was in China, Master Ju-ching of Mt. T'ien-t'ung asked me to be his attendant, saying: "You may be a foreigner, but you're still a man of talent." I declined the offer firmly. My reasons were that, although such a position would do much for my reputation in Japan and be important for my study of the Way, there were monks of insight in the assembly who might criticize a foreigner's being appointed attendant in a great Zen temple, since it would indicate a lack of suitable candidates in China. One should take such criticism into careful account. I conveyed my sentiments to Ju-ching by letter. He recognized my respect for his country and realized that people were certain to feel criticized. He accepted my refusal and did not ask me again.

2

Dōgen instructed:

Someone has said: "I am ill and of small talent and have not the strength to study the Way. Yet I have heard the essentials of the teaching and would like to retire and live alone and spend the rest of my life caring for my body and trying to cure my illness." This is a great mistake.

The old sages did not necessarily have bones made of metal. Were the men of the past all possessed of superior talents? It has not been so long since the Buddha's death, and those who listened to him in his lifetime were not all superior beings. His followers included both the good and the bad. Among them were some whose conduct was unbelievably bad, as well as people of the lowest type. Yet there was none who, claiming inferiority, failed to arouse the mind that seeks the Way. Nor were there any who, saying they had no talent, declined to study the Way. If you do not practice and study in this life, in what life can you expect to gain the talent and the well-being to study the Way? The essentials of study are simply these: arouse the mind that seeks the Way and practice without consideration for your own life.

3
Dōgen instructed:
Students of the Way, do not crave for clothing and food. Each person has his allotted share of food and life. He cannot obtain more than his share even if he tries. Indeed, those who study Buddhism also receive offerings from donors as a matter of course. This cannot be compared with ordinary begging. Monks also have community property that does not require individual effort to obtain. The three types of food, fruit of trees and plants, food gained from begging, and food donated by believers, are the pure foods. Foods connected with the four callings—farmers, merchants, warriors, and artisans—is impure and is not to be partaken of.

Once there was a monk who died and went to the land of death. Yama, King of the dead, said: "This man has not yet exhausted his share of life. Send him back."

One of the officials of hell replied: "Although his share of life is not yet exhausted, his share of food has already been used up."

"Then let him eat lotus leaves," Yama said. After returning to the world, the monk could not eat ordinary food and finished out his life eating lotus leaves.

Thus, students, through the strength gained by studying Buddhism, do not exhaust their share of food. Through the virtue of the curl between the eyebrows of the Buddha[1] and his legacy of twenty years,[2] monks cannot exhaust this food, even though endless eons pass. They must concentrate on training and not seek clothing and food.

From medical science we know that, if the body, flesh, and blood are kept healthy, then the mind in turn becomes well. How much more attuned will the mind of the student become if he can govern his body in accordance with the conduct of the Buddhas and Patriarchs, while maintaining the precepts and living in purity.

Students, when you want to say something, think about it three times before you say it. Speak only if your words will benefit yourselves and others. Do not speak if it brings no benefit. These things are difficult to do all at once. Keep them in mind and learn them gradually.

4

After a talk on a variety of subjects, Dōgen instructed:

Students, don't worry yourselves about clothing and food. Although Japan is a small and out-of-the-way country, it has gained fame in both the exoteric and esoteric schools of Buddhism in the past as well as at present. In later generations it has produced many men of great renown. There have been many who excelled in poetry and music and in literature and the martial arts and who have devoted themselves to their practice. I have yet to hear of one of them, however, who luxuriated in clothing and food. Because they endured poverty, forgot all other things, and single-mindedly pursued their Way, they gained fame. How much less so then should students of the Patriarchal Way, who have discarded the world and abandoned the search for fame and profit, expect to gain material riches!

Although this is a decadent age, in the Zen monasteries of China there are a million students. Among them are some who have come from afar and others who have left their native provinces, and almost all of them are poor. Yet they do not worry about their poverty. They worry only about having not yet attained enlightenment. Wherever they sit doing *zazen,* whether on the top floors or in the lower parts of a building, they practice Buddhism single-mindedly, as though in mourning for their departed parents.

I myself have seen a monk from Szechuan who, coming from afar, had virtually no possessions. All he had were two or three pieces of charcoal, worth perhaps two or three hundred *mon,* the equivalent of twenty or thirty *mon* in Japan. With these he bought a cheap grade of thin paper, out of which he made a coat and a pair of trousers. Every time he stood up you could hear them tear, but his miserable appearance did not bother him in the least.

Someone suggested: "You should return to your home and come back when you are properly clothed and equipped."

The monk answered: "My native place is far from here, and it would take me a long while to make the trip. I would just be spending my time in vain and would worry about the time I would lose in my study of the Way." Without bothering about the cold, he practiced the Way. This is why many great men have emerged in China.

5

Dōgen instructed:

I have heard it said that when the temple on Mt. Hsüeh-feng[3] was established, it was very poor. Either the monks had no food at all, or they subsisted on a mixture of steamed beans and rice. Under these conditions they studied the Way, yet later there were never less than fifteen hundred monks studying there. In the old days monks were like that; we must be this way today.

The decadence of monks is usually connected with wealth and rank. When the Buddha was alive, Devadatta's jealousy was aroused by the daily offering of five hundred cart-loads of provisions.[4] He brought harm not only to himself but also to others. Why should true students of the Way wish to gain riches? The accumulation of large stores, even if they are offerings motivated by pure faith, will undoubtedly set one to thinking about rewarding the donors for their favors. The people of this country will make offerings in order to gain benefits for themselves. To give to someone who approaches with a smiling face is a normal human reaction. But, if you behave so as to please others, it becomes an obstacle to the study of the Way. Just endure hunger and cold and devote yourself solely to the study of the Way.

6

One day Dōgen instructed:

A man of old has said: "You must see it, hear it, gain it." He also said: "If you cannot gain it, you must see it; if you cannot see it, you must hear it." This means that you should see it rather than hear it; that you should gain it rather than see it. If you have not yet gained it, then you must see it. If you have no yet seen it, then you must hear it.

7

On another occasion Dōgen said:

The basic point to understand in the study of the Way is that you must cast aside your deep-rooted attachments. If you rectify the body in terms of the four attitudes of dignity, the mind rectifies itself. If at first you uphold the precepts, the mind reforms itself. In China it is the custom among laymen to show their filial gratitude towards a deceased parent by assembling at the ancestral mausoleum and pretending to weep so earnestly that eventually real tears of grief would fall. Students of the Way, even though they do not have the mind that seeks the Way at the outset, eventually arouse this mind merely by a steadfast love and study of Buddhism.

Students who have been moved to study the Way should merely follow the rest of the assembly in their conduct. Don't try to learn the essential points and the examples from the past right away. It is best, however, that they be fully grasped before you go alone to practice in the mountains or conceal yourself within a city. If you practice by doing what the assembly does, you should be able to attain the Way. It is like riding in a boat without knowing how to row. If you leave everything up to a competent sailor, you will reach the other shore, irrespective of whether you know how to row or not. If you follow a good teacher and practice together with the assembly and have no concepts of the Self, you will naturally become a man of the Way.

Students, even if you gain enlightenment, do not stop practicing, thinking that you have attained the ultimate. The Buddha Way is endless. Once enlightened you must practice all the more. Remember the story of the Lecture Master Liang-sui, who came to study under Ma-yü.[5]

8

Dōgen instructed:

Students of the Way must not put off practice to some later day. They must strive each day and each moment, without wasting any time.

A layman who had been ill a long time came here in the spring of last year and gave me a promise, saying: "If this illness is cured, I vow to leave my wife and children and build a small retreat near the temple to live in. Twice a month I will attend the gathering for repentance of infractions of the precepts, participate in the daily practice, and listen to the teaching. I will spend the rest of my life upholding the precepts to the best of my ability." After that, by taking various cures, he managed to get a bit better but then had a relapse and, lying ill, he spent his days in vain. In the first month of this year, his condition suddenly became critical, and his suffering increased. Because there was no time to transport the materials prepared for the small retreat he had planned to build, he borrowed a room from someone and moved in. Yet within a month or two, he was dead. On the night before his death, he received the Bodhisattva precepts, took refuge in the Three Treasures, and faced the end with equanimity. This was better than if he had been at home and had died maddened by the misery of his love for his wife and children. It would have been best, though, had he left his home last year, when he had come to his decision, lived near the temple, became a monk, and ended his life in the practice of the Way. This has convinced me that Buddhist training should not be put off to some later day.

To think that, because you are ill, you must wait to practice until you are cured betrays a lack of the mind that seeks the Way. Our bodies are made up of a combination of the four great elements;[6] who is there that can escape illness? The men of old did not all have bones of metal. If you only have the determination, you can practice, forgetting all other things. When the body confronts something vital, it habitually forgets the trivial and the petty. Because Buddhism is the vital thing, determine to investigate it for your whole life and determine not to pass your days in vain.

An old Master has said: "Do not spend your time wastefully." If you are trying to cure a disease, but it continues to get worse and the pain gradually increases, determine to practice at a time when the pain has eased somewhat.[7] If you suffer severe pain, determine to practice before the disease becomes critical. If your disease is critical, determine to practice before you die. While curing a disease, the illness sometimes lets up and sometimes worsens. There are times when the disease gets better, even though you do not attempt to cure it; and other times when it gets worse, even if you do attempt a cure. Consider this carefully.

Practicers of the Way, do not think of waiting to practice until you have prepared a place to stay or equipped yourself with robes and bowl. If impoverished people put off practice until they have obtained the robes and bowl, which they are too poor to own now, what will they be able to do when they face death? Therefore, if you wait to train until you have found a place to stay and are fitted out with robes and bowl, you will have wasted your whole life. If it is only because of the lack of robes and bowl, even a layman should not let this stop him but should practice Buddhism if he has the desire to do so. The robes and bowl are only ornaments that all monks are supposed to have. The true practicer of Buddhism does not rely on them. If they are there, then they are there. Do not go out of your way to look for them, and do not think that you are lacking something that you have to have. To have a disease that requires curing and to do nothing about it because you are intent on dying—this is a heretical view. Do not begrudge your life to Buddhism; on the other hand, do not fail to save it if you can. If needed, the use of moxa or medicinal herbs does not become an obstacle to practice. It is wrong, though, to set practice aside and to postpone it until you have cured your disease.

9

Dōgen instructed:

In the middle of the sea, there is a place where great waves rise known as the Dragon Gate. If a fish can pass this place, it turns into a dragon. This is why it is called the Dragon Gate. Yet it seems to me that the waves there are no higher than those in other places, and the water must be just as salty as anywhere else. Strangely enough, though, any fish that passes there becomes a dragon without fail. Its scales do not change; its body remains the same; yet suddenly it becomes a dragon.

The practicing Zen monk can be said to be like this fish. When he enters a monastery, although it may not differ from any other place, he without fail becomes a Buddha or a Patriarch. He eats in the way that others eat, wears clothes in the way that others wear them, and quells his hunger and guards himself against the cold in the way that others do. Yet he has but to shave his head, put on the monk's robe, and eat the stipulated meals at the regulated times, and suddenly he has become a Zen monk. Do not seek afar to become Buddhas and Patriarchs. To enter a monastery or not to enter it is no different from a fish passing or not passing the Dragon Gate.

There is a popular saying: "I sell gold, but there is no one to buy it." This can also be said of the Patriarchal Way. This Way is never begrudged. It is freely offered, but people do not accept it. Attaining the Way does not depend on whether one is inherently bright or stupid; anyone can awaken to the Way. The speed with which the Way is attained depends on zealousness or indolence. The difference between zealousness and indolence is determined by the strength of the will to seek the Way. A weak determination comes from a failure to understand impermanence. Every moment, someone dies; this process goes on endlessly without pause. In this short existence, do not spend your time in idleness.

An old proverb says: "The rat living in the storeroom hungers for food; the ox plowing the field never eats its fill of grass." This means to hunger for food while in the midst of food; to want for grass while surrounded by grass. So it is with man. While dwelling within the Buddha Way, he does not accord with the Way. If he cannot stop the mind that seeks after fame and profit, he will spend his life without finding peace.

10

Dōgen instructed:

Every action of a man well versed in Buddhism shows deep thought, whether that action seems good or bad. This, ordinary people do not understand. One day the Abbot Eshin[8] asked a man to beat and drive away a deer that was eating grass in the garden. At that time someone remarked: "You seem to have no compassion. Why have you begrudged the grass and tormented this animal?"

The Abbot replied: "You do not understand. If I did not chase the deer away, it would soon become accustomed to people. If it came near an evil person, it would surely be killed. That's why I chased it away."

Although chasing the deer seemed to show a lack of compassion, it was motivated by a deep compassion.

11

One day Dōgen instructed:

If someone comes to ask about the teaching or the essentials of practice, the Zen monk must always answer him truthfully. If the person seems to be someone of no talent or is a person just starting out, who has little knowledge and cannot understand, the monk must not reply with an expedient or an untrue answer. The spirit of the Bodhisattva precepts requires that he must answer only with the Mahāyāna teachings, even if the questioner is a Hīnayāna man, who asks of the Hīnayāna Way. This is how the Tathāgata taught during his lifetime. The provisional teachings of expediency are really of no value. The last True Teaching[9] alone has real worth. Don't worry, however, about whether the other person understands or not; just answer the truth. When you look at a person, he should be seen from the standpoint of his true virtue. Don't judge by his outward appearance or his supposed virtue.

In ancient times, a man came to Confucius wishing to receive his teaching. Confucius asked him: "Why do you want to become my disciple?"

The man answered: "When I saw you at Court, you looked noble and dignified. This made me want to receive your teaching."

At this Confucius ordered his disciples to bring out vehicles, luxurious costumes, gold, silver, and other treasures. These he gave to the man, saying: "You did not come to learn from me," and he sent him away.

Dōgen continued:

Uji no Kampaku[10] went to the bathhouse of his palace one day to watch the fire being made. The attendant in charge saw him and said: "Who are you to come to this bathhouse uninvited!" and he chased the Kampaku away. Later, the Kampaku took off the poor clothes he had been wearing and changed to a magnificent robe. When he appeared in all his dignity dressed in his resplendent garments, the bathhouse attendant, who caught sight of him from a distance, fled in terror. The Kampaku then hung his magnificent robe on the top of a pole and did homage to it. When he was asked why he did this, he replied: "Others do not respect me for my virtue. It is only this fine robe that they respect." Foolish people render respect in this fashion. Respect for the words of the *sūtra*s and the teachings is also of this sort.

A man of old has said: "The words of statesmen fill the world, yet the words contain no error. The actions of statesmen fill the world, yet no one is dissatisfied with them."[11] This is because what has to be said is said and what has to be done is done. These are the words and actions of the highest virtue and are the essence of the Way. The words and actions of people in this world are calculated to serve personal concepts and can lead only to blame. The words and actions of Zen monks have been established by their predecessors. Do not hold your own personal views. This is the Way that has been practiced by the Buddhas and the Patriarchs.

Students of the Way must each reflect upon themselves. To reflect on your own body is to reflect on how you should behave with your own body and mind. Zen monks are sons of Śākyamuni; they must learn the style of the Tathāgata. The correct rules for the use of body, speech, and mind can be seen in the actions of the Buddhas who have come before. Each one of you must follow these actions. Even among laymen it is said that clothing should follow established precedents and that words should accord with actions. It is all the more essential then that Zen monks do not make use of personal views.

12
Dōgen instructed:

Students today, when they listen to the teachings, try first to give the impression that they have understood well what they have heard, and they concern themselves with being able to give answers that are to the point. Thus, what they hear just passes through their ears. What this amounts to is that they lack the mind that seeks the Way, because they still possess egoistic views.

First of all, you must forget the Self. After listening carefully to what someone has to say, you should think about it quietly. If you find difficulties or have doubts about something, pursue them to the end. If you understand, you should offer your solutions to the Master again and again. To present what you understand at once shows that you have not listened to the teaching well.

13
Dōgen instructed:

During the reign of T'ai-tsung of the T'ang Dynasty, a foreign country presented the Emperor with a horse that could travel a thousand *li* in one day. The Emperor did not rejoice in the gift, thinking to himself: "If I ride a horse that can cover one thousand *li* and I travel this distance, what use is it if my retainers cannot keep up with me?"

He summoned Wei Cheng and asked his opinion. "I agree with you completely," Wei Cheng replied. The Emperor loaded the horse with gold and silks and had it sent back.

When even an Emperor returns things he cannot use, how much more useless is it for a Zen monk to retain anything other than his robes and bowl! Why accumulate useless things? Laymen who specialize in a certain art find no need to have fields, orchards, and manors of their own. They consider that all the others in the country are their own people and their own family, living on land that belongs to them.

Sō, who held the rank of Hokkyō,[12] left these words for his son: "Just devote all your efforts to the Way that you are following now." Disciples of the Buddha must cast aside all other things and concentrate solely on the Buddha Way. This is the most vital thing for them.

14
Dōgen instructed:

Students of the Way, when you study under a teacher and hear the doctrine, listen with extreme attention, and ask again and again. If you do not ask what should be asked and do not say what should be said, it will be your own loss. The Zen Master always awaits a disciple's question and then gives his reply. Even if you understand something, ask about it several times until you are absolutely sure about it. The Master must ask whether the disciple understands or not and must explain things thoroughly.

15

Dōgen instructed:

The points to watch for those versed in Buddhism differ from those of ordinary people.

When the late Abbot of Kenninji was still alive, there was once an occasion when there was no food to eat at the temple. At that time, however, a parishioner invited the Abbot to call and presented him with a bolt of silk. The Abbot was so delighted that he would not give it to anyone to carry but tucked it into his own clothes and returned to the temple. He handed the silk over to one of the temple officers, saying: "Use this for tomorrow's food."

Just then, however, a request came from a certain layman: "I am embarrassed to ask, but I need two or three bolts of silk badly, and if you can spare any at all, I would deeply appreciate your letting me have some." The Abbot then took back the silk from the officer and gave it to the layman. The temple officer and the other monks were upset by this unexpected action.

Later the Abbot said: "You all probably think that what I did was wrong. But in my view, you have all assembled here with the determination to seek the Buddha Way. To miss a day's food, or even to starve to death, should not bother you. To help ordinary people when they are suffering from want of something will bring excellent benefits to each one of you." This is how someone versed in Buddhism looks at things.

16

Dōgen instructed:

The Buddhas and the Patriarchs were all at one time ordinary men. While in this common state, some were guilty of evil conduct and evil thought, some were dull and others foolish. Yet because they all reformed themselves, followed a good teacher, and practiced, they became Buddhas and Patriarchs. People nowadays must do the same. Don't demean yourself by saying that you are dull and stupid. If you don't arouse the determination to seek the Way in this life, when do you expect to be able to practice? If you force yourself to practice now, you will without fail gain the Way.

17
Dōgen instructed:

A proverb epitomizing the Imperial Way says: "Unless you empty your mind, you cannot accept good advice." This means that, if you cast aside your personal views and follow the advice of loyal ministers, the Imperial Way will manifest itself as it properly should. The epitome of the study of the Way by Zen monks is just like this. If he has personal views even to a small degree, the words of the Master will not enter his ears, and if they do not enter, then he cannot attain to his Master's teaching. It is not enough just to forget the differing views on the teaching, but you must also forget worldly affairs, hunger, and cold. Then when you listen to the teaching, having single-mindedly cleansed both body and mind, you are able to hear with intimacy. When you can hear like this, the principle becomes clear, and doubts are resolved of themselves. True attainment of the Way means to discard the body and mind you have had up to now and just to follow your Master's teaching as it is. If you do this, you will become one truly versed in the Way. This is the most vital truth handed down from the past.

Notes

I

1. The *Biographies of Eminent Monks, Continued,* a work in 30 *chüan* by Tao-hsüan (595–667).
2. The Buddha, the Law, and the Community of monks.
3. The realms of hell, hungry ghosts, and beasts.
4. Unidentified.
5. Eisai (1141–1215) twice visited China and brought back the Zen teachings. He founded the first Zen temple in Japan, as well as the Kenninji in Kyoto. Dōgen was for a while his disciple.
6. The reference here is most likely to the section on the Bodhisattva precepts in the *Brahmajāla Sūtra.*
7. Po-chang Hui-hai (749–814). His work, the *Po-chang ch'ing-kuei,* established the regulations for Zen monasteries.
8. Brought from the West (India) by Bodhidharma.
9. This story is not in the Chōonji edition and may be a later accretion to the text.
10. Title of Cho-an Te-kung (1144–1203).
11. Wu-tsu Fa-yen (d. 1104). He is noted for having produced three famous disciples.
12. This expression is found in a famous *kōan,* known as "Po-chang and the wild fox." It is found in the *Ts'ung-yung lu,* the *Wu-men kuan,* and other works.
13. Reference is to the celebrated *kōan* concerning Nan-ch'üan P'u-yüan (748–834) and the cat.
14. Chao-chou Ts'ung-shen (778–897).
15. The Chōonji text changes the wording slightly and omits a negative here. "When the assembly could not answer, Nan-ch'üan should have paused a while and then said: 'In your silence the Way appears as it is.' "
16. Quoting Yün-wen Wen-yen (d. 949).
17. A phrase that leads to enlightenment.
18. Translation tentative. Texts vary in this passage; the Chōonji version has been followed here.
19. The precepts that lead to emancipation from the evil actions of body, word, and mind.
20. The killing of the cat as a means of bringing enlightenment to others.

21. As given in the section on the Bodhisattva Precepts in the *Brahmajāla Sūtra*.
22. The ten major precepts: not to kill, not to steal, not to be unchaste, not to lie, not to slander, not to insult, not to gossip, not to covet, not to become angry, and not to be skeptical.
23. Shedding the blood of a Buddha; killing a father, mother, monk, teacher, or Arhat; and disrupting the *sangha*.
24. When an evil person is admitted to the assembly he may be treated with a lack of compassion for a while as a means of cautioning him against his past evil.
25. Ju-ching (1163–1228) was the Master of the temple at Mt. T'ien-t'ung. He was Dōgen's teacher.
26. Minamoto no Yoritomo (1147–1199).
27. Rokuhara is a section of Kyoto, east of the Kamo River, in which the headquarters of the Taira family were located. Here the reference is to the head of the family.
28. A famous philosopher-adviser in the Warring States period. A native of Ch'i.
29. Younger brother of the Emperor of Chao. Died 250 B.C.
30. Title of Yung-ming Yen-shou (904–975).
31. The thirty-two marks and the eighty distinguishing characteristics of a Buddha.
32. From a verse by Ch'ang-sha Ching-ts'en (d. 868).
33. The exact meaning of this passage is unclear.
34. *Lun-yü* iv.
35. Two of the ten great disciples of the Buddha.
36. Both were noted beauties of the fifth century, B.C.
37. The names of famous horses.
38. The exact source of this quotation is unknown; possibly it is based on the *Chen-kuan cheng-yao*.
39. The Buddha lived a hundred years, but he entered Nirvana at the age of eighty, offering the remaining twenty years of his life for the benefit of beings in the degenerate age to come.
40. One of the nine distresses suffered by the Buddha during his lifetime.
41. The ninety-day retreat during the summer rainy season.
42. *Wen-hsüan* xxxviii.
43. Brahma, Yama, and other Indian deities, adopted into the pantheon as guardians of Buddhism.
44. Regulations for begging provide that one is to visit seven houses, without concern for whether they are rich or poor.

II

1. Bhaiṣajya, the Healing Buddha.
2. The park near Śrāvastī in which temple buildings were

constructed and where Śākyamuni preached.

3. The second T'ang Emperor, 598–649.
4. The celebrated Minister of early T'ang, 580–643.
5. The first Emperor of the Sui Dynasty, 541–604.
6. Of the Minamoto family. He is reputedly the author of *Kojidan.* He died in 1215.
7. A high-ranking priest of Onjōji, a temple of the Tendai Sect. He later resigned to become a disciple of Hōnen of the Pure Land School. Kōin died in 1216.
8. The Tendai Doctrine holds that each moment of thought has immanent in it the three thousand worlds or all things.
9. A long-nosed demon, variously described.
10. Hung-chih Cheng-chüeh (1091–1157). Noted Zen priest, author of the *Ts'ung-yung lu.* He greatly enlarged the Ching-te Temple at Mt. T'ien-t'ung, where Dōgen was later to study.
11. See chapter 1, sec. 16.
12. The Kōshōji at Fukakusa in Fushimi, south of Kyoto.
13. The Shingon priest Myōhen (1142–1224) from Mt. Kōya. He was converted to the Pure Land teachings, and took the name Kū Amidabutsu.
14. The recitation of the Buddha's name.
15. The period between death and rebirth in a new form.
16. To offer the good that one has done for the sake of others.
17. Representative of the dull and unintelligent disciples of the Buddha. By extreme exertion, he achieved Arhatship.
18. Nan-yüeh Huai-jang (677–744), a disciple of the Sixth Patriarch.
19. Ma-tsu Tao-i (707–786), a disciple of Huai-jang, above.
20. 343?–268? B.C. From the state of Ch'u.
21. The night is divided into five periods of two hours each, beginning at eight o'clock. Each period is divided into five parts of twenty-four minutes each. Here the time is given as the third part of the third period, or about 1:12 A.M.
22. The four forms of demeanor—walking, standing, sitting, and lying—which, when properly exercised, inspire respect.
23. The Chōonji text makes the following a continuation of Ju-ching's own words, rather than a quotation of another priest's remarks.
24. Ling-yün Chih-ch'in gained enlightenment on seeing plum blossoms in bloom. Hsiang-yen Chih-hsien was awakened on hearing the sound of a tile striking bamboo.

III

1. See chapter 1, sec. 14.
2. Hai-wen Shih-chai. Dates unknown. He was Abbot of Mt. T'ien-t'ung shortly before Dōgen's arrival at the temple.

3. Unidentified.
4. The meditation hall was divided into two sections, with a statue of Manjusri in the center. That section that faced the front gate was the front meditation hall; the one that faced the rear gate, the rear meditation hall.
5. 759–824. The story appears in *Ch'ing-te ch'uan-teng lu* xiv.
6. The hole of a bird that nests in the ground. To be bound by delusions.
7. A bucket lacquered black so that one cannot tell what it holds. Delusions.
8. P'ang Yün. High official of the T'ang, celebrated as a lay follower of Zen.
9. Ts'ao-ch'i is the name of the mountain on which Hui-neng (d. 713), the Sixth Patriarch, had his temple.
10. Huang-p'o is the name of the mountain on which the temple of Hung-jen (601–674), the Fifth Patriarch, was located.

IV

1. d. 775. An heir of Hui-neng, the Sixth Patriarch.
2. Apparently, a priest who attended at services in the Imperial Court, attired in a purple robe. Hui-chung, being a National Teacher, officiated at services there.
3. The six sense organs, their objects, and their perceptions.
4. His biography is unknown. He is famous for teaching the "one-finger Zen."
5. January 28, 1327.
6. *Shuza.* The first seat in the meditation hall. The director of the meditating monks, who sometimes preached in place of the head priest of the temple.
7. Bodhidharma, traditionally a priest from India, was the First Patriarch of Zen in China.
8. The Second Patriarch of Zen and the first native Chinese Patriarch.
9. Zen. The term is drawn from the *Diamond Sutra.*
10. Feng-yang Shan-chao (947–1024).
11. Yao-shan Wei-yen (751–834).
12. See chapter 2, sec. 26.
13. A famous *kōan* involving T'ung-shan Liang-chieh (807–869).
14. Quotation from the *Huai-nan tzu.*
15. A work in ten *chüan;* the book is a sort of compendium of political advice. It is apparently the source for several of Dōgen's cautionary remarks on Chinese worthies.
16. Dōgen lost his father at three and his mother at eight, and, while still a child, became an acolyte at the Tendai stronghold of Mt. Hiei, near Kyoto.

17. Men such as Dengyōdaishi, Kōbōdaishi, and Jikakudaishi.
18. The Chinese "Biographies of Eminent Monks" and its sequel.
19. Of action, thought, and words.
20. A famous general of the Warring States period. Parts of the following story appear in *Shih chi* lxxxi.
21. The Buddha divided the teaching of the Law into three periods: 1) the True Law (*shōhō*), the five hundred years after the Buddha's death, when the true teaching would still prevail; 2) the Simulated Law (*zōho*), the one thousand years in which just the teaching and practice would remain but without enlightenment; 3) the Degenerate Law (*mappō*), in which the teaching alone would remain. This period would last ten thousand years. The number of years each period lasts differs in various texts; the above figures, however, seem to have been those accepted in Japan in Dōgen's time.
22. The Chōonji text adds two clauses here: "True Buddhism is not like this. If one practices according to the teaching, one will gain enlightenment without fail." This justifies Dōgen's statement that the Three Periods of the Law are "temporary expedients" and serves to refute the belief that in the "Degenerate Age" no one can attain enlightenment.
23. Unity of body, words, and mind; the same maintenance of the precepts, the same views, and the same practice.
24. Yang-ch'i Fang-hui (992–1049).
25. Lung-ya Ch'ü-tun (835–923).
26. One of the thirty-two marks of a Buddha.
27. Ichijō Motoie (1132–1214). He became a monk at Kenninji in 1201. Jimyōin is one of his pseudonyms.

V

1. First Emperor of the Han, reigned 202–190 B.C.
2. The first unifier of China, d. 210 B.C.
3. See chapter 2, sec. 23.
4. Reference is to the story of Po-i and Shu-ch'i, two legendary brothers who rejected a kingdom and retired to Mt. Shou-yang, where they starved to death.
5. Known also as Le-t'an K'o-wen (1025–1102).
6. Hsüeh-feng Tao-yüan. Dates unknown, a fellow disciple of K'o-wen under Huang-lung Hui-nan. The present edition gives Yün-feng as the name of the mountain associated with this priest. It has been changed to Hsüeh-feng, following the Chōonji edition. Both Yün-feng and Hsüeh-feng are mountains that housed temples famous in Zen.
7. A disciple of Fen-yang Shan-chao (947–1024). He died at the age of ninety-two, sometime between the years 1056 and 1064.

8. Myōzen (1183–1225) was a disciple of Eisai and was Dōgen's teacher for a period. He went to China with Dōgen and died there.
9. Details of his life are not known.
10. 596–664. Celebrated priest who journeyed to India in search of the scriptures. He translated a large number of texts and was a leader of the Consciousness-only School.
11. Drawn from the *K'ung-tzu chia-yü,* a collection of quotations from a large variety of early Chinese works. The authenticity and authorship of the work extant today are subjects of scholarly dispute.
12. A work in 100 *chüan,* translated by Kumārajīva. It is a commentary on the *Prajñāpāramitā Sūtra.*
13. Ta-hui Ts'ung-kao (1089–1163). One of the most famous Zen Masters of the Sung Dynasty.
14. A famous verse, widely used in Zen, attributed to Seng-ts'an, the Third Patriarch.
15. Reference is to a story of the Buddha before he had gained his enlightenment. He experienced such joy at the sight of a certain ancient Buddha that for seven days he recited verses and uttered words of praise, forgetting either to pick up or put down his feet in the interim.
16. The five evil monks who were too lazy to read the *sūtra*s and, as a result, who received no offerings. They made a show, however, of practicing meditation and received support but eventually fell into hell. They were reborn as imperfect beings, such as stone women.
17. From a *kōan* concerning Chao-chou Ts'ung-shen.

VI

1. One of the thirty-two marks of a Buddha.
2. See chapter 1, sec. 16.
3. Reference is to the temple of Hsüeh-feng I-ts'un (822–908), a famous Zen Master of the T'ang Dynasty.
4. Devadatta was Śākyamuni's cousin and is representative of the evil men who tried to thwart the Buddha's purpose. His crimes were so numerous that he fell into hell while still alive. Jealousy over the 500 cart-loads of provisions, offered by a wealthy donor, motivated Devadatta to commit his evil acts.
5. Liang-sui, a Buddhist scholar who lectured on the scriptures, visited Ma-yü Fa-ch'e and gained enlightenment under him. Later, Liang-sui stopped giving lectures, dismissed his disciples, and devoted himself to his own study of the Way. Ma-yü was a disciple of Ma-tsu Tao-i. His dates are not known.
6. Earth, water, fire, and wind.

7. The Chōonji text changes this sentence somewhat: ". . . the pain gradually increases, you will wish that you had practiced when the pain was still light."
8. Otherwise known as Genshin (941–1003). A famous priest of the Tendai Sect, he lived at Yokawa on Mt. Hiei, near Kyoto.
9. Reference is to the teachings of the *Lotus Sutra* and the *Nirvana Sutra*. In the Tendai doctrine, these represent the highest of the five grades of teaching preached by the Buddha.
10. Reference is to Fujiwara no Yorimichi (992–1074). He built the famous Byōdōin at Uji as a family temple. *"Kampaku"* is a title, the equivalent of Regent or civilian dictator.
11. Quoted from the *Book of Filial Piety* iv.
12. A high priestly rank. "Sō" is presumably a proper name. It appears as Chisō in the Chōonji text. He cannot be identified.